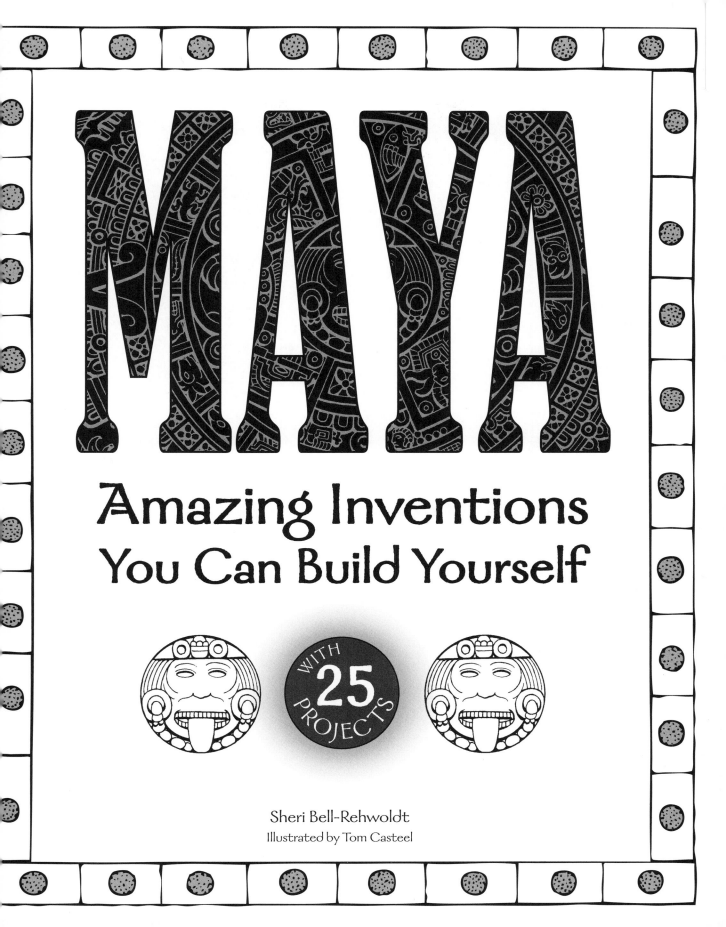

MAYA

Amazing Inventions
You Can Build Yourself

WITH **25** PROJECTS

Sheri Bell-Rehwoldt

Illustrated by Tom Casteel

~ Titles in the *Build It Yourself* Series ~

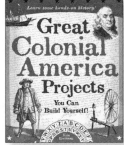

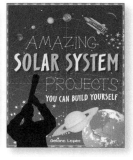
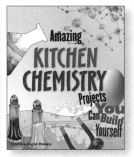
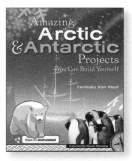

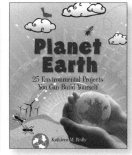

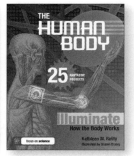

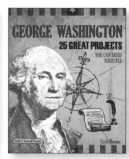

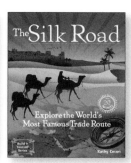

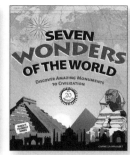

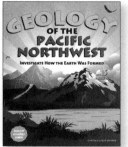

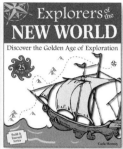

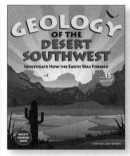

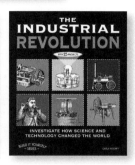

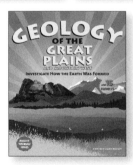

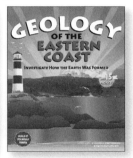

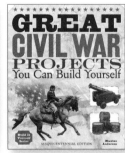

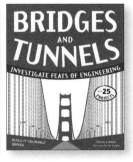

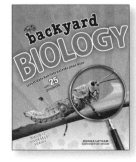

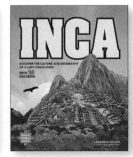

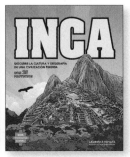

green press
INITIATIVE

Nomad Press is committed to preserving ancient forests and natural resources. We elected to print *Maya: Amazing Inventions You Can Build Yourself* on 4,007 lbs. of Williamsburg Recycled 30% offset.

Nomad Press made this paper choice because our printer, Sheridan Books, is a member of Green Press Initiative, a nonprofit program dedicated to supporting authors, publishers, and suppliers in their efforts to reduce their use of fiber obtained from endangered forests.

For more information, visit **www.greenpressinitiative.org**

This book was manufactured by Sheridan Books,
Ann Arbor, MI USA.
June 2012, Job #336308
ISBN: 978-1-936749-61-4

Illustrations by Tom Casteel
Educational Consultant, Marla Conn

Questions regarding the ordering of this book should be addressed to
Independent Publishers Group
814 N. Franklin St.
Chicago, IL 60610
www.ipgbook.com

Nomad Press
2456 Christian St.
White River Junction, VT 05001
www.nomadpress.net

CNTENTS

IMPORTANT DATES: Timeline of the Maya

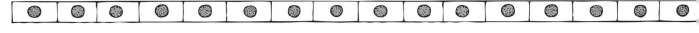

The ancient Maya civilization lasted about 3,000 years. Its history is divided into three main time periods: the **pre-classic period**, the **classic period**, and the **post-classic period**. Descendants of the Maya still live in Central America.

2000 BCE–250 CE (pre-classic period): Evolution from hunter-gatherers to farming villages to great cities.

700 BCE: Mayan written language is developed.

400 BCE: Olmec civilization begins to decline.

100 BCE: City of Teotihuacán is founded.

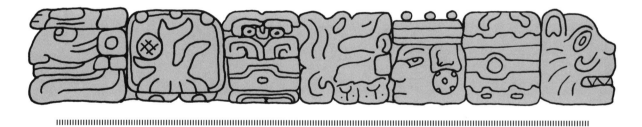

250 CE–900 CE (classic period):
Known as the *golden age*. Maya kings rule great cities.

450 CE: Teotihuacán is at its peak as the center of a powerful Mesoamerican culture.

500 CE: Many citizens of Teotihuacán flee to Tikal, which becomes the first great Maya city.

600 CE: A mysterious event destroys Teotihuacán. Tikal becomes the largest city in Mesoamerica.

683 CE: At age 80, the greatest Maya king, Pacal II dies.

751 CE: Trade between city-states declines and conflict increases.

869 CE: Tikal begins to decline and is abandoned in 899.

IMPORTANT DATES: Timeline of the Maya

900 CE–1600 CE (post-classic period): Maya flee their southern lowland city-states. Cities in the northern Yucatán continue to thrive until they are conquered by the Spanish.

1224 CE: City of Chichén Itzá begins to be abandoned, and people settle outside the city.

1263 CE: The people of Chichén Itzá build the city of Mayapán, which becomes the capital of Yucatán.

1441 CE: The people of Mayapán start to leave and the city is abandoned by 1461. After this, warring groups compete to rule over the others.

1502 CE: Christopher Columbus learns of the Maya. Spanish conquistadors set out to claim the resources of the land and people.

1519 CE: Hernán Cortés explores the Yucatán and the Spanish begin their conquest of Mexico.

1541 CE: The Spanish conquer the Maya and establish a capital city at Mérida in the northern Yucatán.

1562 CE: A Spanish bishop brutally forces the Maya to accept Catholicism.

1695 CE: The ruins of Tikal are discovered by a Spanish priest who had become lost in the jungle.

1697 CE: The last ancient Maya city, Tayasal, falls to conquistador Martín de Ursúa.

1843 CE: John Lloyd Stephens and Frederick Catherwood explore Central America looking for Maya ruins. They publish a book of their travels, sparking world interest in the ancient Maya.

1886 CE: Mayan hieroglyphs begin to be catalogued.

1952 CE: Pacal II's tomb is discovered at Palenque.

1973 CE: Scholars make breakthroughs in understanding the Mayan written language.

1992 CE: Rigoberta Menchú, a Maya woman, wins the Nobel Peace Prize for fighting for human rights for the Maya.

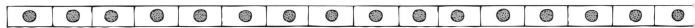

Pacal the Great

Pacal II: The most famous Maya king, also known as Pacal the Great, or K'inich Janahb' Pakal. Ruler of the great Maya city-state of Palenque for 68 years, from age 12 to age 80. The name Pacal translates to "shield." After his death he was worshipped as a god.

Shield Jaguar the Great: King of Yaxchilán, a rival city of Palenque, from 681. He died at age 92 in 742 CE. A powerful warrior, he brought many other cities under his control.

Lady Xoc of Yaxchilán: The most prominent wife of Shield Jaguar the Great, Lady Xoc is shown in many Yaxchilán stone carvings.

Waxaklajuun Ub'aah K'awiil: Also known as 18 Rabbit, he was the 13th ruler of Copán and one of the city's most famous kings. He ruled from about 695 to 738 CE, when he was captured and sacrificed by a rival king.

Hernán Cortés (1484–1547): The conquistador who left Spain in 1519 to capture Mesoamerican gold for Spain.

Charles V, King of Spain (1500–1558): Approved the Spanish conquest of the Americas, after taking the throne in 1516.

Diego de Landa (1524–1579): A Spanish priest who tried to brutally convert the Maya to Christianity by burning the Maya codices, torturing Maya people, and demolishing Maya buildings.

John Lloyd Stephens (1805–1852) and Frederick Catherwood (1799–1854): Published a book in 1843 about their discovery of the Maya ruins, which sparked interest in the Maya among archaeologists, scholars, and the general public that continues today.

Hernán Cortés

IMPORTANT PLACES: Geography of the Maya

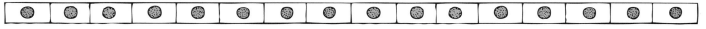

Yucatán Peninsula: The heart of Maya civilization.

Teotihuacán: A powerful Maya city until 500 CE.

Tikal: The first great city of the Maya civilization.

Palenque: A great city ruled by Pacal the Great.

Yaxchilán: An important city in the classic period.

Copán: A strong kingdom established with an unusually wealthy citizenship.

Uxmal: A city that dominated all of the northern Maya area for generations.

Chichén Itzá: A major city around 600 CE.

Mayapán: A pre-Columbian political capital in the Yucatán Peninsula from the late 1220s to the 1440s CE.

Tayasal: The last Maya city-state to be subdued by the Spanish, in 1697 CE.

Mérida: The modern capital city of the Yucatán state in Mexico.

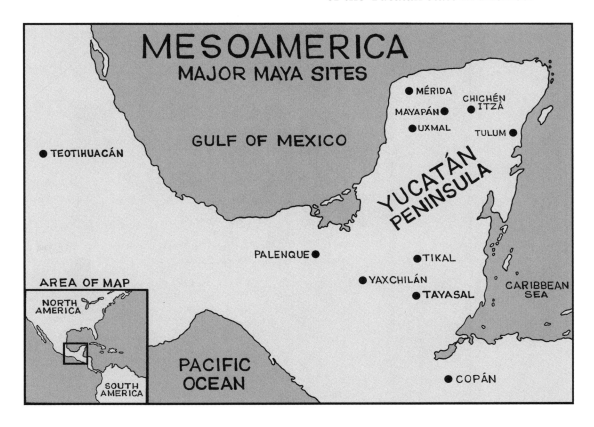

INTRODUCTION

Have you ever thought about what life was like during the time of the ancient Maya, long before the first European explorer set foot in the New World?

The ancient Maya people were the most advanced **civilization** of their time. They are known as accomplished mathematicians and master builders of huge cities. They are also famous for their complex written language and calendar system, and for creating some of the world's most impressive jewelry, carvings, paintings, and ceramics.

Zero   One   Two   Three   Four   Five

This book will help you learn about the Maya's fascinating calendars and **hieroglyphics**. How did they raise crops in poor soil and create a vast network of huge cities? You'll discover that the Maya people believed their gods created the world's first humans—and demanded blood **sacrifices** in exchange for this gift of life! You'll explore how the Maya built towering pyramids from slabs of **limestone** and carved intricate patterns into hard green **jadeite** stone. By the end of this book you'll see what daily life was like in Maya society.

Most of the projects in this book can be made with little adult supervision, and the supplies for each are either common household items or easily available at craft stores. So, take a giant step back—into the time of the Maya—and get ready to Build It Yourself!

WORDS TO KNOW

civilization: a community of people with a highly developed culture and social organization.

hieroglyphics: a type of writing system that uses pictures and symbols called hieroglyphs (or just glyphs) to represent words and ideas.

sacrifice: an offering to a god.

limestone: a kind of rock the Maya used to build roads, temples, and other important buildings.

jadeite: a rare and prized mineral, usually emerald to light green.

DID YOU KNOW?

"Maya" or "Mayan"? The term "Mayan" should be used only when referring to the Mayan language. The term "Maya" should be used when you talk or write about the people and their culture. Maya is both singular and plural.

   2

ONE

Uncovering an
ANCIENT LEGACY

**Deep in the rainforests of Central America
sit the ancient ruins of a people called
the Maya (pronounced MYE-uh).**

For over 3,000 years, the Maya lived in an area of about 125,000 square miles, in what are now the countries of Mexico, Belize, Guatemala, El Salvador, and Honduras (over 300,000 square kilometers). At their peak, as many as 10 million or more Maya lived in this area, which historians call "Mesoamerica."

In 1843, explorers John Lloyd Stephens and Frederick Catherwood published a book about the Maya ruins. This is how people became aware of the once-great cities that existed.

When Stephens and Catherwood found the ruins of the ancient Maya city Copán, they gazed in awe at its towering pyramids and tall stone **stelae** carved with hieroglyphs. Amazingly, Stephens was able to buy the ruins for $50 so that he and Catherwood could study them in detail.

Catherwood spent many hours sketching copies of the hieroglyphs in his notebooks. He was sure the symbols told about Maya life. When **epigraphers** and **archaeologists** saw Catherwood's drawings, they knew he was right. Soon, scholars around the world began to study the ancient Maya. A strong interest in Maya history continues today.

DID YOU KNOW?

Catherwood used a drawing device called a camera lucida that allowed him to see the object he was drawing and his paper at the same time. He was able to easily trace the outlines of buildings and stelae, ensuring that his drawings were accurate.

A Close Call for Catherwood

In 1839, Stephens, an American travel writer, and Catherwood, a British architect, traveled to Central America. They had heard of fantastic old ruins. Their exploration wasn't easy: it was hot in the **tropics**, the mosquitoes were fierce, and monkeys howled in the treetops overhead. They also battled **malaria**.

At the ruins of the Maya city Palenque, Catherwood caught malaria. The disease attacks red blood cells, causing them to burst. Symptoms include fever, shivering, vomiting, and joint pain. Catherwood did recover and he returned to Central America with Stephens, where they discovered the Maya ruins of Chichén Itzá and Tulum. When Catherwood got sick again, both men returned to New York to publish a book called *Incidents of Travel in Yucatán*. The book describes the 44 Maya sites Stephens and Catherwood found during their expeditions.

Who Were the Ancient Maya?

Scholars still have much to learn from the Mayan glyphs and ruins. But they have uncovered enough information for us to answer the question, "Who were the ancient Maya?"

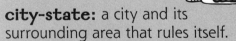

WORDS TO KNOW

tropics: near the equator.

malaria: a painful tropical disease caused by mosquito bites.

city-state: a city and its surrounding area that rules itself.

The Maya were one of the great civilizations of the Americas. But there was not one single Maya empire. The Maya were spread among a group of **city-states** that were independent and ruled separately, but shared a common culture. Maya city-states shared similar religious beliefs, social structures, and building styles to other Mesoamerican cultures like the Olmec and Aztec, but each civilization was unique.

BCE? CE?

What does it mean when dates end with the letters BCE and CE? BCE stands for Before the Common Era. The beginning of the Common Era is marked by the birth of Jesus and begins with the year 1 followed by the letters CE. Events that happen before the first year of the Common Era are Before the Common Era. The years BCE may seem backward, because as time passes the years actually become smaller in number. For example, a child born in 300 BCE would celebrate turning 10 in the year 290 BCE. Think of it as a countdown to the Common Era. ⌇

Experts divide Maya history into three time periods:

- **pre-classic period**, 2000 BCE–250 CE
- **classic period**, 250–900 CE
- **post-classic period**, 900–1600 CE

Maya society grew from simple beginnings. Long before they lived in great cities, the Maya were **nomads**. They roamed the land in small family groups, moving to new areas when they ran out of food. Between 2,000 and 4,000 years ago, as the Maya learned to harvest **maize** and other **crops**, they began to build small villages and settle in Mesoamerica.

WORDS TO KNOW

nomads: a group of people who move in search of food and water.

maize: corn.

crop: plants grown for food and other uses.

DID YOU KNOW?

The word "Maya" most likely came from the city Mayapan, which was considered the last great Maya capital in the period prior to the Spanish conquest. When the Spanish needed a word to refer to the people of the newly conquered province of Yucatán, they chose "Maya."

As the farmers spread across the region, they faced many challenges. In the south, near the highland mountains (now Guatemala and Honduras), they found volcanic soil good for growing crops. But in the northern lowlands of

the Yucatán Peninsula, only 2 inches of soil covered solid limestone. Yet this scrubby area flowed with many underground streams and wells the Maya called *dz'onot*, and which the Spanish later called *cenotes*.

• •

The Maya believed these wells led to the
underworld, the home of evil gods.

• •

The farmers that settled in the central and southern lowlands were surrounded by thick, tropical rainforest. They grew cotton, despite the heavy rains that fell from May through December, when the waters could rise 10 feet or more (3 meters). But the animals of the forest, such as monkeys, jaguars, iguanas, deer, turkeys, wild boar, and birds, provided the Maya with plenty of food. Maya who settled along the coast traded salt, turtles, fish, and oysters for crops they couldn't grow.

WORDS TO KNOW

Pok-A-Tok: a ball game in which teams acted out the ongoing battle between good and evil.

Around 500 BCE, the Maya began to transform their central lowland villages into great cities. Some of these cities included Palenque, Tikal, and Yaxchilán. Later, the Maya also built cities in the south and east. One of the most impressive is Copán, the first city Stephens and Catherwood found. By 50 CE, pyramids, city plazas, and **Pok-A-Tok** ball courts were added to the cities.

By 300 CE, the cities were divided into four classes of people. At the top were the kings, priests, and other members of the royal family. In the middle were the merchants and artists. Below them were the *memba uinicoob*, which means "common worker." The lowest class of people was the slaves, called *pentacoob*. Maya kings enjoyed unlimited wealth and power, while slaves had nothing and were even used for human sacrifices.

DID YOU KNOW?

The *memba uinicoob* were the workers in each city's population. It was their job to build the city structures and roads. They also built the stone homes of the royals and planted their crops.

 8

WORDS TO KNOW

debt: a service or money owed.

obsidian: a black glass produced by erupting volcanoes.

flint: a very hard, grayish-black form of quartz.

The ancient Maya were a Stone Age people, meaning they did not have metal tools to help them with their daily tasks. Their tools were made of wood, stone, and bone. Instead of iron-tipped arrows, chisels, knives, axes, and hammers, their wooden tools had blades made from **obsidian** and **flint**. Both could be chipped to make sturdy, razor-sharp blades.

Groups of Maya People

ajaw: lord.

halch uinic: the leader or king of each Maya city who held his position for life, and passed it on to his son.

bataboob: the nominated local leaders and officials who were members of the noble class.

ppolm: merchant traders.

memba uinicoob: common workers, who made up most of the Maya population.

pentacoob: the Mayan word for slaves, a group that included people in **debt**, criminals, and war prisoners. ເວ

The Maya Golden Age

We know the most about the Maya classic period (250–900 CE), as this was the Maya golden age. It was during these years that the Maya reached their greatness as a society. Cities grew strong, and skills and knowledge flourished.

Archaeologists have found ceramic objects, wall paintings, and jewelry that show the artistic skills of the ancient Maya. Experts have also discovered Maya books, called **codices**, which prove that the Maya wrote down every syllable they spoke. This was just one accomplishment that set them apart from their Mesoamerican neighbors.

Another factor that set the Maya apart was their knowledge of mathematics. The ancient Maya developed a counting system based on the number 20. The system used "steps" to increase numbers by **multiples** of 20. This allowed the Maya to calculate into the millions. They were also the first people to use zero as a place holder.

WORDS TO KNOW

codice: an ancient writing in book form.

multiple: a number that can be divided evenly by another number.

conquistador: a sixteenth-century Spanish soldier.

Smart ideas, however, couldn't keep Maya cities from collapsing. Around 750 CE, the southern lowland cities began to fail. By 1000 CE, many sat empty and abandoned. Archaeologists aren't sure why the Maya left their cities. But most experts believe the populations of the cities became too great for the amount of food farmers could produce. Residents left the cities when they began to starve.

In 1502, Christopher Columbus captured a Maya trading canoe near the Gulf of Honduras. Word spread to Spain about the rich cultures of Mesoamerica, which attracted Spanish **conquistadors** in search of gold. This led to the downfall of both the Aztecs and Maya.

Other archaeologists believe common workers left the cities when they got tired of working for their kings. Or maybe the Maya fled their cities because of disease, earthquake, and war. Experts agree that most of the ancient Maya living in the southern lowlands likely died within a short time period. The rest moved to cities in the northern lowlands of the Yucatán Peninsula. These northern cities remained strong until the Spanish conquistadors invaded the Maya homeland and forced the Maya to be their slaves.

DID YOU KNOW?

Skeletons dating from around 850 CE show that the Maya living in the southern lowlands suffered from starvation and diseases like malaria and yellow fever.

Who Were the Aztecs?

By 1325 CE, the Aztecs had completed construction of their huge capital city, Tenochtitlán, built on an island. The city had more than 50,000 residents living on corn, beans, chili peppers, squash, tomatoes, and tobacco. After the collapse of the Maya cities, the Aztecs ruled much of southern and central Mexico. Like the Maya, the Aztecs believed their gods demanded blood sacrifices. To have success in war, the Aztecs sacrificed many victims at the same time by removing their hearts.

The Aztecs were known for their gold jewelry, and in 1519, conquistador Hernán Cortés led more than 500 soldiers into Aztec territory in search of gold. At first the Aztecs thought Cortés was a god, so they gave him great respect and their gold. But they attacked Cortés and his men when they saw their gold being loaded onto ships headed for Spain. In 1521, the Spanish took control of Tenochtitlán, and Aztec society quickly ended. Today, Mexico City is built over its ruins.

Spanish Conquistadors

The Spanish sailed to Central America to claim gold for their king. One of the first conquistadors to arrive was Hernán Cortés, in 1519. After Cortés took all of the gold from the Aztecs, the Spanish looked to see what they could take from the Maya. When they didn't find gold, they took their land instead.

The Maya fought back, but they were no match for the conquistadors. Why were the Spanish able to conquer the Maya?

First, the Spanish had better weapons. The Maya fought with spears and arrows, while the conquistadors used canons, guns, metal weapons, and horses. The Maya had never even seen horses before! Written records mention how surprised the Maya warriors were when the Spanish jumped off their wounded horses to keep fighting. The Maya had assumed the horses and riders were a single being.

Second, the Maya and the conquistadors had very different war strategies. The Spanish saw war as a way to destroy their enemies and take their goods. The Maya, though, believed that life was sacred, and murder a crime. Even before killing an animal to eat it, Maya hunters thanked it, saying, "I have need." They viewed blood sacrifice the same way—as a necessary part of the life cycle.

Third, the Spanish brought new diseases to the Maya, which killed millions of them. These diseases included measles, chicken pox, and smallpox. And finally, Maya priests had predicted that Maya cities would fall before a foreign enemy, and so many of the Maya simply gave up when the Spanish attacked them.

WORDS TO KNOW

colonist: a new settler in an area who is originally from somewhere else.

ancestor: a person from your family who lived before you.

By 1547, the Spanish had made slaves of many Maya, except those who fled into the rainforest. The Spanish also tore down many Maya cities so they could build new Spanish cities for their **colonists**, who took the best Maya farmlands. They forced the Maya to grow new crops for Spain, including onions, garlic, wheat, cumin, oregano, cinnamon, rice, olives, limes, bananas, coffee, and sugar cane.

The Maya Today

Though their grand cities have been abandoned, the Maya people have not disappeared. Today, around 10 million Maya and perhaps more, live in the same regions of Mexico, Guatemala, Belize, El Salvador, and Honduras as their **ancestors**. More than half of Guatemala's population is Maya. Some cities, such as Mérida and Cancún in Mexico, have large populations of Maya. Most, however, live in rural areas, but still do not own their own farmland.

Like their ancestors, today's Maya are not one group. Their many populations share a cultural history, but each has its own traditions, languages, and customs. By holding on to their unique ways of life, the Maya have shown incredible strength and character in facing all of the challenges thrust upon them in the modern world. There are still many native Mayan languages, but most Maya today speak Spanish.

KINGS AND PRIESTS

Unlike their Aztec neighbors, the ancient Maya people were not ruled by one king. Each Maya city had its own king. The ancient Maya called these kings *halach uinic*, which means "true man."

Kings: Life and Death

Some ancient Maya cities remained small, but others grew and joined to form large city-states. This happened when kings captured enemy kings, or when royal families in different cities were united through marriage. Some city-states had more than 50,000 residents.

WORDS TO KNOW

commoner: an ordinary person without rank or title.

rival: a competitor.

raid: attack.

Why did residents work hard and without complaining to help keep their cities strong? Because Maya **commoners** believed in putting their king and city first. It was the king's job to bring good fortune to the city. The Maya respected their kings, believing the gods liked the kings best and that the kings spoke directly to the gods. In return for the king asking the gods to bless their city, workers worked hard for the king. If crops failed, however, or disease spread through the city, the Maya believed the gods were punishing them—or their kings. This was a good time for **rival** kings to attack.

Anyone who didn't obey and serve the king was enslaved or killed. The Maya could also become slaves if they were captured by a rival city during a war **raid**, if they were sold by their families to pay off a debt, or if they were caught stealing. Anyone caught stealing a second time would be killed in order to rid the city of the thief's evil spirit.

DID YOU KNOW?

It was easy to tell who the Maya slaves were. They had short haircuts, and their bodies were often painted in black and white stripes.

WORDS TO KNOW

headdress: an elaborate covering for the head worn during ceremonial occasions.

pelt: an animal skin.

behead: to cut off a head.

Slaves were highly valued by the royals, not only because they did so much work, but also because they made for good sacrifices to the gods! Sometimes priests and royals bought slaves from trade merchants just for this purpose.

Maya artists often painted pictures of kings sitting on their thrones. These kings usually had at least one bodyguard nearby to protect them against surprise war raids. Warriors usually attacked rival cities at night, suddenly announcing their presence by blowing a loud horn. Dressed in tall **headdresses** and animal **pelts**, warriors carried flint-tipped wooden spears and shields woven from palm leaves or animal skins. And their wives traveled with them! War raids could last several weeks and were never held when it was time to plant or harvest crops, as this source of food was critical to all of the city-states.

Maya kings feared being captured, tortured, and **beheaded** by a rival king as part of a blood sacrifice. One famous Maya king who met this fate was Waxaklajuun Ub'aah K'awiil, whose name translates to "18 Rabbit." From about 695 to 738 CE, 18 Rabbit ruled the city of Copán. His head was chopped off by Cauac Sky, the king of a rival city-state.

When commoners died, they were buried beneath the floor of their simple mud houses with their personal items. A jadeite bead was placed in their mouths to prepare them for rebirth in the next world.

• • • • • • • • • • • • • • • • • • •
Kings got a much more elaborate send-off.
• • • • • • • • • • • • • • • • • • •

WORDS TO KNOW

majestic: of impressive beauty.

luxury: something that is nice to have but is not necessary.

quetzal bird: a bird prized by Maya kings for its brilliant blue-green feathers. Today this bird faces extinction.

They were buried in **majestic** tombs, with enough clothing, weapons, and slaves to serve them in the afterlife. Even favorite dogs were buried with them! Before their bodies were sealed in tombs, the kings were adorned in pieces of jadeite jewelry. Pacal II, the great king of Palenque, was buried with a jadeite burial mask that covered his entire face.

Kings faced stress and danger, but they also enjoyed many **luxuries** such as dressing in jaguar pelts, fancy jewelry, and the beautiful tail feathers of the **quetzal bird**. And they got to live with their families and advisors in beautiful stone palaces.

DID YOU KNOW?

▶◀▶◀▶◀▶◀▶◀▶◀▶◀▶◀▶◀▶◀▶◀▶◀

With so many residents to feed, kings often fought over croplands. But war raids were also held to steal people for slavery and human sacrifices.

The Quetzal Bird

The quetzal bird is a member of the trogon bird family, and it is similar to the road runner. They nest in trees and holes throughout the jungle, and they have striking feathers. Because the quetzal bird was considered to be sacred and their feathers were so beautiful, only kings were allowed to wear them. ⌁

Priests: Royalty and Healers

Like the kings, priests were highly respected by city residents. Many priests were members of royal families. It was their job to communicate with the gods and make important decisions about when crops should be planted, when women should have babies, and when special religious ceremonies should be held. They made these based on the movements of the planets, moon, and stars. **Scribes** wrote down their calculations.

WORDS TO KNOW

scribe: a member of Maya society who wrote with hieroglyphs on many types of surfaces, as well as in codices, to keep records of all kinds.

Maya priests kept track of time by watching the skies. They used only a forked stick and their eye to track the movements of stars and planets. They were even able to calculate when the planets would align and when solar eclipses would occur. They recorded this **astrological** information in codices.

WORDS TO KNOW

astrological: relating to movement of the planets, moon, and stars.

The Maya believed their gods moved the planets and considered Venus to be the most important of all. They called it *"Nok Ek,"* which means "Great Star," because it was so bright that it was visible to the naked eye. They also thought the planet was linked to their serpent god *Kukulcán*, and Maya kings went to war based on its position. Priests made predictions about the future when Venus appeared. They believed the night skies told them the best days for couples to marry and have children, what children should be named, and when human sacrifices should take place.

Death & Burial

Though death was a common part of their lives, the ancient Maya feared their own deaths. They considered an "ordinary" death to be the worst way to die because they believed that dying from disease or old age meant spending an eternity in the cold and unhappy underworld. The honor of living in paradise, they believed, was only given to warriors who died in battle, to women who died in childbirth, and to those killed in sacrifice.

Shaman-priests were skilled doctors. They were different from regular priests in that they took care of the physical needs of the people. To heal the sick, they used magic, sorcery, and medicines made from plants and the natural world. They made potions from animal **dung**, urine, crocodile and rooster testicles, bat wings, and live toads. They also prescribed steam baths and used herbs, such as leaves and juice from the **agave** plant, to brew healing teas. Today, medical researchers study ancient Maya remedies.

WORDS TO KNOW

shaman-priest: a priest-doctor in Maya society who tended to the physical needs of the people.

dung: solid waste.

agave: a type of cactus plant that grows in Mexico and Central America. The Maya used it for its sisal fibers.

demon: an evil spirit.

DID YOU KNOW?

The ancient Maya believed sickness was caused by **demons**. To make the demons happy, the Maya left food out for them. Today, the Maya still follow this practice.

When seeing a sick patient, the first thing the shaman-priest did was try to figure out the cause of the illness by throwing animal bones on the ground and "reading" them. Shaman-priests offered sacrifices to gods they thought might be angry. Sometimes they even bled the body part that hurt the patient, to get rid of any evil spirits. If someone suffered from headaches, a shaman-priest might make cuts in the forehead.

Maya Matchmaker

Shaman-priests were more than just healers. They blessed ceremonies that were important in the daily lives of the ancient Maya. These included the coming-of-age ceremonies held to publicly announce that the boys and girls were no longer children. Together with official matchmakers, called *atanzahab*, shaman-priests also helped arrange marriages. The *atanzahab* checked that the stars predicted good luck for the bride and groom and made sure the groom paid a fair price for his bride.

After a wedding feast, the groom moved in with his wife's family for five to seven years. After that, the couple moved permanently into or nearby the home of the groom's family. Kings often had more than one wife, but common people could only have one spouse at a time. ᥫ᭡

DID YOU KNOW?

The Maya believed in ending unhappy marriages, and divorce was common. If either person wanted to remarry after the divorce, they skipped the matchmaker and wedding ceremony.

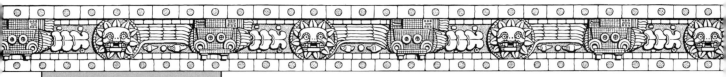

SUPPLIES

pencil

heavy construction paper or poster board

fine-tip paintbrush

Elmer's glue

plastic container and spoon for each sand color

different colors of colored sand, available in craft stores

hair spray or artist's fixative

Make Your Own
SAND ART PICTURE OF THE COSMOS

Maya priests were experts at studying the sky. Make your own model of the celestial bodies they relied on to make important decisions for all members of their society.

1 Use a pencil to draw a picture of the stars and planets on the construction paper or poster board. Remember that really small shapes are hard to fill in with sand. Decide where you want to put each sand color, and write the first letter of the color where it should go.

2 With your paintbrush, apply an even layer of glue to a small section of your design. It's important to work on small sections so the glue doesn't dry out before you cover it with sand.

3 Use the plastic spoon to pour a small amount of the colored sand onto the glue. You can spread it out with your finger, if necessary. Hold your paper over the sand container and tap it so the excess sand slides back into the container. You can also put all the excess sand in one container to make multicolored sand.

4 Repeat these steps until your entire design is finished. Let it dry. To "set" your sand painting, lightly spray it with hair spray or artist's fixative.

 22

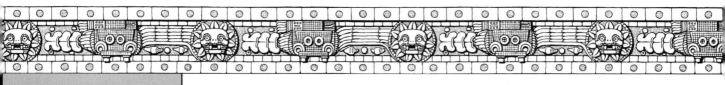

SUPPLIES

wax paper or newspaper

3-D craft plastic facemask (sold in craft stores) OR gallon-size milk jug

X-acto knife or scissors

green tissue paper or green-colored pages from old magazines

watered-down white glue or decoupage solution

foam brush

black and white paint

paintbrush

Make Your Own
ROYAL "JADEITE" BURIAL MASK

This activity will teach you to appreciate the beauty and color of the burial masks favored by Maya kings. *If you use an X-acto knife, please have an adult supervise this activity.*

1 Lay out your wax paper or newspaper and place the plastic facemask face up on your surface. If you are using a milk jug, cut the jug in half at the seam with the X-acto knife or sharp scissors. You can use the side with the handle for a good nose shape.

2 Lay sheets of the green paper on top of each other and cut or tear the stack into strips and then into a variety of shapes. Each piece becomes a "jadeite" tile. If you are using magazine pages, select as many different shades of green as you can find.

3 If using glue: Use your foam brush to add a thin layer of glue to a small section of your mask. Cover the glue with your paper tiles. Continue this process until the entire mask is covered in several layers of "jadeite." Allow the mask to dry overnight.

4 If using decoupage solution: Use the brush included in the bottle to cover a small section of the mask. Cover with the paper tiles. When done, brush a final coat of the decoupage solution over the finished mask. This will give it a hard finish. Allow the mask to dry overnight.

5 Paint white ovals to make eye sockets. When the white paint is dry, paint round black circles in the ovals for the eyeballs.

  23

THREE

CHAPTER 3

Gods and
SACRIFICES

Every aspect of Maya culture was based on religion. The Maya were polytheists, which means they worshipped many gods. Maya experts know that the Maya had names for at least 166 gods, and maybe more.

WORDS TO KNOW

polytheist: a person who believes in more than one god.

fetish: a small figurine believed to have magical or spiritual powers.

The Maya made small figurines of their gods called **fetishes**, which they prayed to every day. They also offered their gods blood sacrifices in exchange for favors. The Maya usually sacrificed animals like dogs, turkeys, squirrels, and iguanas. But humans were sacrificed during large community ceremonies held for important requests like good crops.

Perhaps the Maya spilled blood so easily because they believed their gods had done so first. According to Maya legend, the first humans were created when the gods mixed their blood with maize.

For this gift of life, the Maya believed their gods expected blood offerings in return. Without blood sacrifices, the Maya feared the gods would get angry and destroy the world.

Important Maya Gods

Hunab-Ku: supreme god believed to have created the world.

Itzamná: god of the heavens, who introduced the Maya to writing, farming, and medicine.

Chaac: god of agriculture, rain, and lightning.

Kinich-Ahau: god of the sun.

Yum-Kaax: god of corn.

Ixchel: goddess of fertility and childbirth.

Yat Balam: god of war.

Ek-Chuah: god of merchants and selling.

Ah-Puch: god of death who ruled over Mitnal, the land of death.

The Maya also offered blood sacrifices to keep the world from spinning out of control. They believed gods guided the sun and moon across the sky each day. When the earth was cloaked by night, the gods led the sun on a journey through the underworld, threatened by evil gods. The gods leading the moon fought a similar battle during the day. In order to have the strength to win this daily battle, the gods needed human blood sacrificed by the Maya. Because priests and kings had the most access to the gods, they were expected to offer up their own blood.

• •

The ancient Maya believed that their god Itzamná,
which translates to "Iguana House,"
gave humans writing, farming, and medicine.

• •

One of the most famous records archaeologists have discovered of royal blood sacrifices is a carving of Lady Xoc, wife of a Yaxchilán king known as Shield Jaguar. He was a powerful warrior who brought many cities under his control. In the carvings, made around 725 CE, Lady Xoc is shown asking a god to give Shield Jaguar victory in battle. She is pulling cords with thorns through her tongue as Shield Jaguar holds a flaming torch above her. She would have completed this painful act after **fasting** for days, then eating plants that put her into a **trance**. When she had covered strips of bark with her blood, she would have burned the strips. The Maya believed the gods appeared in smoke as it spiraled skyward.

WORDS TO KNOW

fasting: to eat very little or nothing at all. The Maya usually did this for religious purposes.

trance: a sleeplike state.

procession: a group of people moving along in the same direction, to the same place, or for the same reason.

During large community sacrifice ceremonies, the kings communicated with the gods in public. Community residents also played important roles. Men and women danced separately in group dances. They played instruments in complicated musical **processions**. Written records from this period note that the participants were severely punished if they stepped out of beat or hit the wrong note.

Maya Universe

The Maya believed the universe was divided into three layers. The upper layer contained the stars and was the home of the sky kings. The middle layer was the earth. The lower level was the underworld or *Xibalba*, which translates to "place of awe." This was the home of evil gods. The center of the earth, from which the world tree sprouted, was green. The Maya called this tree *wakah-chan*, which means "raised-up sky." Its branches supported the sky, but its roots burrowed deep into the underworld.

The Maya believed the earth was flat with four corners. At each corner, there was a jaguar of a different color, each representing a compass direction, holding up the sky. The jaguar in the east was red, the jaguar in the north was white, the jaguar in the west was black, and the jaguar in the south was yellow. According to the Maya, the Jaguar god inhabited the underworld, home of the dead, but each morning he became the Sun god, who traveled across the sky from east to west, then returned to the underworld every evening. 〜

The Maya turned to nature for their instruments. For trumpets, they blew into **conch shells,** or carved them from long **gourds** or wood. They also made rattles from gourds. They hollowed out logs and covered the ends with deerskin to make drums, or made them from large turtle shells and used deer horns for drumsticks. They even made flutes out of clay and the leg bones of deer.

To purify themselves for the sacrifice ceremonies, kings and priests washed themselves carefully and refused to eat. The priests then painted their bodies blue—the color of water and sky—and painted their sacrificial victims blue as well. The priests made this paint by blending **indigo** dye and clay.

During religious ceremonies the priests and kings wore special ceremonial masks and headdresses decorated with the feathers of toucans, parrots, pheasants, and **curassows**. These feathers represented the gods the priests and kings were trying to contact. The Maya believed that by putting on the headdresses, the priests and kings became the very gods they were trying to look like. The ceremonial headdresses were often taller than the kings and priests and included a front piece carved to represent one or more of the gods.

Kings also wore ceremonial belts made from leather, cloth, and **sisal** rope that were decorated with shells, beads, and large rectangular pieces of green jadeite, sometimes carved into the shape of human skulls. Some kings chose to wear real human skulls on their belts!

WORDS TO KNOW

conch shell: a large spiral shell that can be used as a horn.

gourd: the dried and hollowed-out shell of plants related to the pumpkin, squash, and cucumber.

indigo: a blue dye made from the indigo plant.

curassow: a long-tailed, crested bird that is found in Central and South America.

sisal: stiff fibers from the agave leaves used by the Maya to make rope and for weaving.

Agave

In addition to making rope, sisal fibers from the agave plant were used to make everyday items such as baskets, sleeping mats, fans, hats, and shoes. The agave is a cactus with needle-sharp spines. Its leaves can grow as long as 6 feet (2 meters)! When the pulp of these leaves is removed by pounding or pressing, tough strands of sisal fibers remain. The agave plant depends on a specific type of moth to pollinate it. This moth is very important because if it doesn't stuff pollen balls into the cup-shaped stigma of each flower, the plants can't reproduce. But what's really interesting is that the moth is just as dependent on the plant. Without agave seeds to eat, the moth caterpillars would starve after hatching! ⬿

When ready to conduct the sacrifices, the priests and kings climbed the steps of their steep pyramids to reach their sacred temples. Unlike the triangle-shaped pyramids in Egypt, Maya pyramids were flat on top. The Maya believed their pyramids represented mountains, and the temples at their top were caves. At this height, the Maya felt closest to their gods living in the sky world. Kings and priests had to master the skill of climbing the temple steps on only the balls of their feet since the steps were so narrow.

DID YOU KNOW?

Most tourists who climb up and down the pyramids today walk sideways. Many even climb down from the top sitting down, step by step. It is so steep that many people get dizzy.

The Maya word for pyramid is *witz*, which means "mountain." The Maya believed mountains housed the souls of their ancestors and gods. To be close to them, the priests placed ceremonial altars at the top of their pyramids.

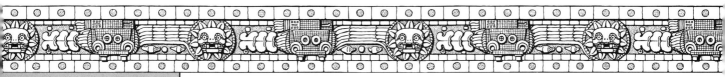

SUPPLIES

balloons

newspaper

Celluclay instant papier-mâché powder and water

scissors

½ cup dried beans or rice (about 100 grams)

stick (long and thick enough to serve as your gourd rattle handle)

hot glue gun

brown, black, yellow paint

paintbrush

spray varnish

twine

beads (with holes large enough for the twine to go through)

feathers

Make Your Own
MUSICAL GOURDS

The Maya invented musical instruments based on the natural world. Here are two ways to make a musical gourd. The second method (on next page) makes a more authentic Maya maraca, but you need time to dry out the gourd. *Have an adult help with the hot glue.*

1 Blow up a balloon to form your "gourd" and tie a knot. Cover your work surface with newspaper.

2 Mix the Celluclay powder with water, following the directions on the packaging. Build up the shape of your gourd by applying the clay with your hands. Evenly cover the entire balloon, then set it aside to dry.

3 Cut a hole slightly larger than your stick in one end of the "gourd" and pop the balloon. Pour about a half cup of dried beans or rice (or both) into the hole.

4 Carefully slide the stick into the hole so that it goes in about 2 inches (5 centimeters). Have an adult help you hot glue the stick into place and seal the hole. This also stops your beans or rice from spilling out. Allow the glue to dry.

5 Paint the gourd brown and then add texture by adding squiggly lines or speckles with your black and yellow paints. Allow the paint to dry.

6 Spray the gourd with at least one coat of varnish to make it shiny. Hot glue twine strands around the handle. Hang beads and feathers from the ends of the twine. As you shake the rattle, they'll jump around.

  31

Method 2 on next page . . .

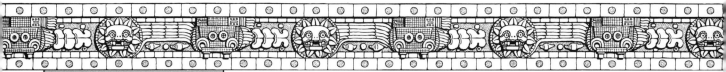

SUPPLIES

gourd—try to find one
that has a long neck,
or natural "handle"

sharp knife

spoon

scissors

twine or string

feathers, shells, beads

hot glue gun

dry beans, rice, or gravel

Make Your Own
MUSICAL GOURDS

Method II

This project is simple but lots of fun. *You will be using a sharp knife and hot glue, so ask an adult to supervise.*

1 Hold your gourd by the handle. Have an adult help you use the sharp knife to chop off the top of the gourd where it starts to widen. You'll be gluing the top back on to the gourd, so try to make a clean cut and set it aside.

2 Use your spoon to scoop out the gourd's insides. Let the gourd dry out for a few days. The drier it is, the better the sound will be.

3 Cut several pieces of twine or string approximately 4 inches long (10 centimeters). Attach feathers, shells, or beads to the strings. Leave about 1½ inches of each string free (about 4 centimeters).

4 Take the hot glue gun and glue the free end of the strings to the inside of the gourd. The end of the strings with the feathers and beads will hang over the outside of the gourd.

5 When the strings are glued in place, fill the inside of the gourd with a handful of dry beans, rice, or even gravel. Don't pack the gourd full—allow room for the beans to shake around.

6 Use the hot glue gun to glue the handle of the gourd back on the body of the gourd. When it is dry you'll have a beautiful Maya maraca!

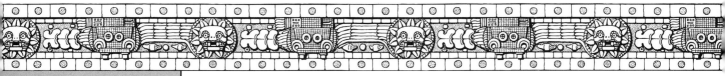

SUPPLIES

wax paper

Sculpey clay—black, tan, white, brown, and green

toothpicks

small green beads

medium black or brown beads

small rectangle of foil

plastic knife

Make Your Own
CLAY GOD FETISHES

These are traditional fetishes you can make yourself. Once you get the hang of it, you can also choose an item or symbol that is important to you in your daily life and make your own version of a Maya fetish. *Have an adult supervise while you use the oven to bake your figures.*

Part I: Iguana

1 Spread out your wax paper on your work surface. Using the brown or green clay, roll a ball of clay into a log about 4 inches long (10 centimeters). At one end of the log, push the sides of the clay together to form a triangle shape. This is your iguana's head.

2 Use your toothpick to make two holes for the eyes. Place two small green beads in the holes.

3 Make a long curved tail from the other end of the log. Make legs by rolling two medium balls of clay into thin logs. If you curve the legs, your iguana will appear to be moving.

4 For more decoration, insert a row of beads down the iguana's backbone. Bake according to the directions on the clay wrapper.

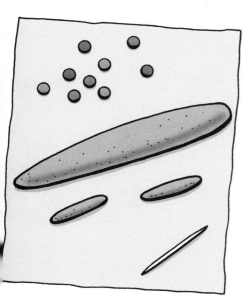

 33

Activity continued on next page . . .

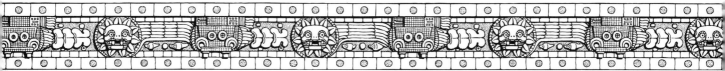

Make Your Own
CLAY GOD FETISHES

Part II: Human Face

1 Cover your work space with wax paper. Roll out the black Sculpey clay to form a thin 2-inch square (5 square centimeters).

2 Wad the foil up to form an oval 1 inch across (2½ centimeters). Roll out either the tan or white Sculpey to make a rectangle about 1½ inches across (4 centimeters). Cut a long oval piece out of the rectangle. This becomes your god's head. Drape the head over the piece of foil so that it is rounded like a real person's face.

3 Lay the head with its foil stuffing on the flat black square and push them together gently. Trim the black clay so that it is only slightly larger than the head. You can cut the edges straight, or make them wavy or zig-zagged.

4 Using the leftovers of your white or tan clay, make 3 little logs. These become the mouth and eyes of your god. Also make a small triangle. This becomes the nose of your god. Attach the eye logs to the middle of the head. Then push the nose and mouth into place. Lay a toothpick across the eyes and gently push down. This forms upper and lower eyelids.

5 Add eyeballs by placing 2 green beads between the eyelids. Make 2 small holes at the bottom of the nose to create nostrils. Place the brown or black beads around the top of your god's head to create hair.

6 Bake according to the directions on the clay wrapper.

FOUR

MERCHANTS

Like kings and priests, trade merchants also played a critical role in society. They bought and sold food and other items all over Mesoamerica.

Food, Gems, and CHOCOLATE!

Merchants from the lowlands traveled to other cities to sell honey, cotton cloth, tobacco, vanilla, **cacao** beans, and animal skins. Jadeite, obsidian, **copal**, and the quetzal feathers worn only by kings came from the highlands. Merchants from the coastal cities sold dried fish, turtle eggs, shells, pearls, and salt. All of these merchants preferred to peddle their goods in busy city squares.

Often, merchants traveled west for long distances to trade with their Toltec and Aztec neighbors. On land, they carried their goods on their backs, using a **tumpline**, as they didn't have horses or other pack animals. With a tumpline, the Maya could carry loads weighing as much as 70 percent of their body weight.

WORDS TO KNOW

cacao: beans containing seeds that are used to make cocoa, cocoa butter, and chocolate.

copal: a kind of sap that comes from tropical trees that is used in candles.

tumpline: a sling for carrying a load on the back, with a strap that passes around the forehead.

The Maya Invented Chocolate Drinks!

The word chocolate is said to come from the Mayan word *xocoatl*. The Maya farmed cacao trees just so the kings could have their favorite frothy chocolate drinks whenever they wanted.

Cacao trees grow in the damp shade of Central American rainforests. Each tree sprouts flower blossoms that must be fertilized by tiny gnats before they become seed pods. The Maya dried the beans, ground them up, and mixed them with water. Then they poured the mixture from one drinking jar to another to make it foamy. When Spanish soldiers arrived, they grew to love the taste of cacao, adding sugar to their chocolate drinks to make them less bitter. They shipped the beans back to Spain and the Spanish royal families fell in love with the drink, too.

Today, factory workers harvest cacao pods. They split each hard pod open with a heavy wooden hammer and remove the 40 or so beans, which are surrounded by sticky, white pulp. Beans are dried in the sun, and then roasted at a high temperature to bring out their flavor. A special machine separates the shell of the bean from the inside of the bean, which is called the nib. The nibs are ground until they turn into a thick paste. This paste is used to make your favorite candy bars!

DID YOU KNOW?

In the 1920s a man in Mexico City delivered pianos on his back using a tumpline.

Maya traders also crossed rivers and the ocean to reach the Caribbean and Panama. To do so, they used large wooden canoes called *chem*. The Maya carved *chem* from the trunks of mahogany and other hardwood trees. At more than 40 feet long (12 meters), the canoes could carry up to 20 people!

Cacao (pronounced ka-KOW) was so valuable, it became the **currency** of the Maya. Why? Kings loved to have frothy chocolate drinks made from cacao seeds! Common workers couldn't drink them

WORDS TO KNOW

currency: money or other valuable item used for exchange.

because they couldn't afford them. Some traders tried to fool buyers with fake beans. These dishonest men filled empty bean pods with sand. Everyone soon learned to test the beans to make sure they were solid by biting them.

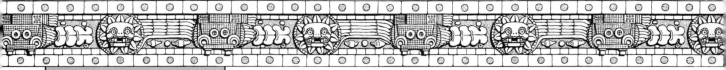

SUPPLIES

saucepan

2 cups milk
(about 500 milliliters)

4-ounce-disk pressed
dark bitter Mexican
chocolate (a popular
brand is "Ibarra")

whisk

2 drinking cups

Make Your Own
MEXICAN HOT CHOCOLATE

Treat yourself like royalty and mix up a tasty chocolate drink. *You will be using a hot stove, so have an adult supervise this activity.*

1 Warm the milk and chocolate in a saucepan over low heat. Use a whisk to mix the chocolate into the steaming milk. Remove the hot mixture from the stovetop.

2 To froth the milk, stir hard with the whisk. Or, you can do what the Maya did to froth their chocolate drink: pour the milk from one cup to another until it fills with air bubbles. Serve it in two cups.

DID YOU KNOW?

Written records found by archaeologists tell us that an adult male slave could be bought with 100 cacao beans.

Farming, Food, AND CLOTHING

The common workers (*memba uinicoob*) of Maya societies enjoyed few luxuries in life. They lived in simple mud houses and worked hard all day. Unless on a war raid, the men were either planting and harvesting crops, or building pyramids and roadways. The main crop of the Maya was maize, what we call corn. Farmers also grew black and red beans, squash, pumpkins, chili peppers, tomatoes, avocados, papayas, and sweet potatoes.

  39

Food and Farming: Few Tools, Little Water

Maya commoners went to bed early as a family, sleeping together in the same room. In the morning they rose before dawn, so the men could get to the fields before the day got hot. Without metal tools or machines, they used pointed sticks to dig holes in the ground for their crop seeds. There were no horses to help them plow the fields so farming was slow and difficult work.

Corn was a spiritual crop to the Maya, as it symbolized birth and death. The Maya worshipped Yum-Kaax, the god of corn.

During the Maya classic period (250–900 CE), farmers developed some smart ways of farming. In low swampy areas, for example, they built raised fields. They tucked flat **terraces** into hillsides to prevent the soil from washing away during rains. And they rotated their crops every couple of years so the soil had time to rest between plantings.

Yum-Kaax, Maya god of corn.

DID YOU KNOW?

The Maya created chewing gum, which they called *cha*. They took the thick, milky sap that oozed out of the wild sapodilla tree, waited until it hardened, and then chewed it.

In areas without rivers, the ancient Maya did something really inventive: they dug **reservoirs**. A reservoir is like a giant bowl that collects rainwater. An ancient Maya reservoir can be found in the ruins of Tikal, a city in northern Guatemala. Tikal was surrounded by 10 reservoirs, each of which held up to 40 million gallons of water (150 million liters)! In places where they had too much water, the Maya built canals and **aqueducts** to channel water through the cities. You'll see an old aqueduct if you visit the ruins of Palenque.

WORDS TO KNOW

reservoir: a natural or artificial pond or lake used to store and regulate the supply of water.

aqueduct: a pipe or channel designed to transport water by force of gravity from one place to another.

drought: a long period of little or no rain.

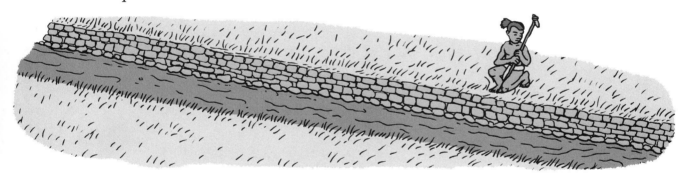

As creative and successful as the Maya farmers were when it came to collecting and channeling water to their crops, during **drought** periods their reservoirs and aqueducts were sometimes in danger of drying out. During these periods, it is believed that the Maya would make musical instruments to encourage rainfall for their crops. Rainsticks are hollow tubes with pins stuck through them, filled at one end with small beads or beans. When one side of the stick is upended, the beads inside fall to the other end of the tube, and as they bounce off the pins, they sound a lot like a rainstorm.

Making Tortillas Is Hard Work!

The Maya did not use forks or spoons. They used tortillas! Rolled up, the tortillas worked like spoons for sauces and beans. It took a lot of tortillas to feed everyone in the family this way—and a lot of effort to turn dried corn into flat tortillas. Every night, women set dried corn kernels to soak in a pot of water and lime to soften them. At around four in the morning, the women got up to grind the softened corn into flour and make dough. Then they were ready to make their tortillas. After building fires under their three-stone **hearths**, Maya women patted the dough into patties and baked the day's tortillas one at a time.

WORDS TO KNOW

hearth: the floor of a fire or oven.

gnarled: twisted and deformed.

The Maya ate corn tortillas at every meal. Corn had to be ground fresh daily because it didn't keep well in the humid climate. Women used a grinding stone called a metate, which is a slab of rock about 1 foot wide and 18 inches long (30 by 45 centimeters). They pushed a stone tool that looks like a rolling pin, called a metapil, over the corn kernels until they were ground to a fine flour. They then mixed the flour with water to make dough. Experts know that Maya women spent a lot of time on their knees grinding corn because the knee bones of the skeletons of Maya are **gnarled**. Knee bones of the skeletons of royal women, however, are not gnarled because they had slaves to do the work.

Clothing: Traditional Weaving

While men were busy in the fields, women worked hard at home. They made the tortillas and tended their home gardens and beehives, took care of children, prepared all the family meals, and wove cloth. The looms used by ancient Maya women were called backstrap looms because one end was tied around a tree and the other was tied around the weaver's back.

Backstrap looms were small and **portable**. They could be used anywhere there was a tree or post. Ancient Maya codices show images of Maya women using backstrap looms. Two thousand years later, the Maya still view the backstrap loom as a sacred symbol and continue to use it to weave cloth.

WORDS TO KNOW

portable: able to be carried around easily.

DID YOU KNOW?

The goddess lxchel was said to have invented backstrap weaving.
She is the goddess of medicine, childbirth, and weaving.

To make thread from their cotton crops, Maya weavers used a tool called a **spindle whorl**. With one hand they twirled a foot-long stick (30 centimeters), weighted and balanced by a disk near its bottom, and fed cotton fibers to the stick with the other hand. As the cotton twisted, it made thread. Then, the weavers colored the thread with vegetable and mineral dyes, and wove colorful cloth. Commoners wore simple clothing. Men wore a **loincloth** called an *ex* and women wore loose, embroidered dresses called *huipils* and a light shawl called a *pati*. It took Maya women two or three months to weave a *huipil*.

WORDS TO KNOW

spindle whorl: a rod or pin, narrow at one end and weighted at the other, on which fibers are spun into thread and then wound.

loincloth: a strip of cloth worn around the midsection of the body.

· ·

Women still wear *huipils* in Guatemala and Mexico today.

· ·

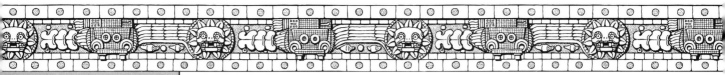

SUPPLIES

2 cups corn flour
(260 grams)

1 cup warm chicken
broth (250 milliliters)

½ teaspoon salt

mixing bowl

wooden spoon

glass bowl

plastic wrap

rolling pin

frying pan or skillet

stove

tin foil

fillings, such as
cheese and salsa

Make Your Own
HOMEMADE TORTILLAS

Tortillas are still served at most meals in Mexico today. The ancient Maya warmed their tortillas on a stone over a fire, but you can make tortillas in your modern-day kitchen. *Have an adult supervise as you cook the tortillas on the stove.*

1 Mix the three ingredients with a wooden spoon to form a dough. On a lightly floured surface, knead the dough until it is no longer sticky. This will take about 5 minutes.

2 Put the dough in a glass bowl and cover it with plastic wrap. Let the covered bowl sit on the counter for about an hour.

3 Divide the dough into 12 equal pieces. Remove one piece at a time from the covered bowl, as the plastic wrap will keep the remaining dough from drying out.

4 Form each piece of dough into a ball with your hands and then flatten it between your palms. Use your fingertips to stretch the dough into a thin circle or roll it with a rolling pin between two pieces of plastic wrap.

5 When your tortillas are nice and flat, get your parents to help you fry them in the skillet at medium-high heat. Flip the tortilla to brown both sides. Put them in tin foil to keep them warm.

6 Hot tortillas taste good with many different fillings, like shredded cheese and salsa. Roll them up and enjoy!

  45

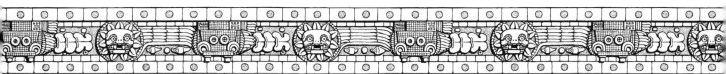

SUPPLIES

empty wrapping paper or paper towel tube

fine-point black marker or pen

60 or more 1-inch nails (2½ centimeters)

heavy-duty tape (masking, packing, or duct tape)

construction paper

scissors

rubber bands

rice or small, uncooked beans

paint, markers, or other decorations

Make Your Own
RAINSTICK

You may live in an area where there is plenty of rain for your home garden, but the sound of these rainsticks is lovely anytime! *Have an adult supervise since you will be using nails.*

1 Use a fine-tipped black marker or pen to draw dots about a half-inch apart (about 1½ centimeters) all the way down the spiral seam of the cardboard tube.

2 Poke a 1-inch nail all the way in at each dot (2½ centimeters). Make sure that you don't poke through the other side of the tube! You will need about 30 nails for each foot of cardboard tube.

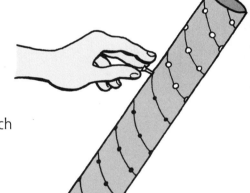

3 After you have finished poking in all the nails, carefully wrap the tape all the way around the tube to hold the nails in place.

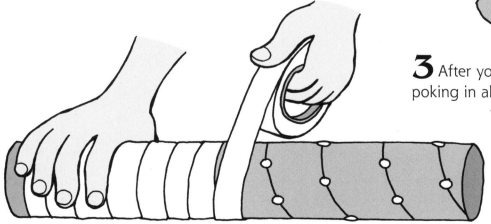

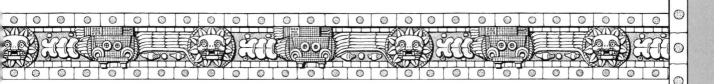

4 Cut 2 circles of construction paper just a little bigger than the ends of the tube. Put one of the paper circles over one end of the tube and secure it with a rubber band. Cover the circle and rubber band with tape so the whole end of the tube is sealed shut.

5 Put a handful of rice or beans into the open end of the tube. Cover the open end with your hand, and turn the tube over to hear the sound of your rain stick. Add or remove rice or beans until you have the sound you like. Beans will make a louder sound while rice will make a softer sound.

6 Place the second circle of paper over the open end of the tube, secure it with a rubber band, and seal that end with tape. Decorate your rain stick however you like.

7 Turn your rain stick over again and again. Shake it, tap it, and enjoy the sound!

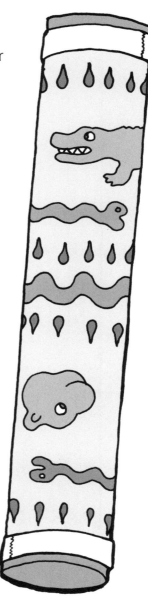

DID YOU KNOW?

The Maya believed that flint produced sparks because it contained the spirit of lightning.

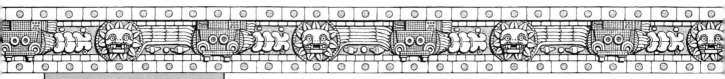

Make Your Own
LOOM AND CLOTH

This activity gives you a sense of how much work it was for Maya women to weave clothing by hand for an entire family.

1 Cut the top (or flaps) off of a cardboard box. Using your ruler and a pencil, mark every ¼ inch on two opposite sides of the cardboard box (about every ½ centimeter). Make sure that the marks on one side line up with the marks on the other side. Then make 1-inch cuts on each of the marks (2½ centimeters).

2 Next you need to string your warp, or the lengthwise strings of the weaving. Secure the end of your string to the bottom or side of your cardboard box (your loom) with a piece of tape. Slide the string into the first cut on one side and gently pull it across the loom and into the corresponding cut on the other side. Wrap the warp thread around the bottom, pulling the thread into the next cut on the other side of the box edge. Continue to wrap the warp around the box until all cuts are full. Tighten any loose threads to an even tension, and then secure the other end of the warp string on the bottom or side with a piece of tape.

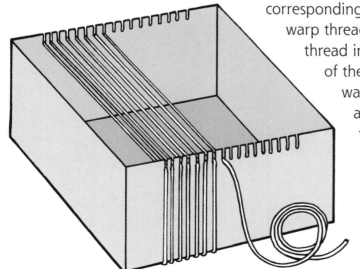

 48

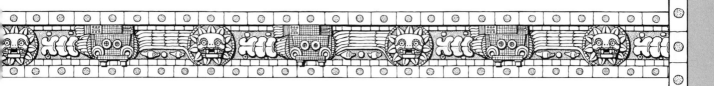

3 Now your loom is ready for weaving! Choose the yarn you want to start with and tie one end to the first warp string. Wrap the other end of the yarn around your pencil. Put a piece of tape around the pencil to secure the yarn.

4 Push the pencil under the first warp string and over the next all the way across until you have woven all the strings. Begin the second row by weaving back toward the direction you just came from. Note that you must weave the second row the opposite way from the first row, going over the warp strings that you just went under, and under the warp strings you just went over.

5 To change the color or texture of the yarn as you are weaving, tie one end of the new yarn to the end of the old yarn, and the other end of the new yarn to the end of the pencil. Make sure the knot is pushed to the back of the weaving. After every couple of rows, pull all the yarn gently to make sure that the fabric is tight and even. Just be careful not to pull it too tightly or your fabric will not have straight edges.

6 When you have woven your fabric and completely filled up the loom, you can finish off your cloth by tying the yarn to the very last warp string. Then cut all warp threads from your cardboard loom and tie pairs of strings on each side together in a tight knot to finish off your cloth.

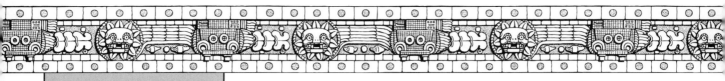

SUPPLIES

wooden model car wheel, about 2 or 3 inches in diameter (23 centimeters) (available at most craft stores)

wooden dowel that will fit snugly into the wheel's center hole

ruler

pencil

serrated knife

electric pencil sharpener

cotton inserts from vitamin jars or bundle or raw cotton from a yarn store

Make Your Own
MAYA SPINDLE WHORL

Spinning yarn will take some practice, but this whorl will help you learn how skilled the Maya were at this craft. *This activity uses a sharp knife, so ask an adult for help.*

1 Using a ruler, mark 9 inches from the end of your wooden dowel (23 centimeters). Ask an adult to carefully saw through the dowel at the mark with the serrated knife.

2 Push the dowel through the hole in the car wheel far enough so 2 inches of the dowel are below the wheel (5 centimeters).

3 Using an electric pencil sharpener, sharpen each end of the dowel into a point.

4 Sit on the floor with your legs crossed like the ancient Maya. You can rest the whorl in a small bowl to help keep it in place when you spin it. Moisten the pointed top of your spindle whorl with your tongue. Hold your spindle whorl in your right hand and the cotton in your left hand. Poke the top of the whorl into the edge of the cotton, spinning the whorl to the right (clockwise) until some of cotton fibers catch.

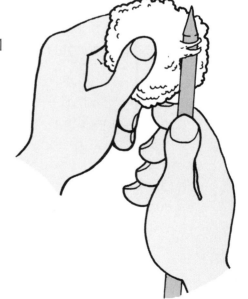

5 As you spin the whorl with your right hand, it should be at a slight bend to the left, close to a 45-degree angle. Use your left hand to gently pull the cotton fibers up and away from the spindle tip. Cotton fibers are very short, so don't pull on the cotton too hard or the fibers will pull apart completely. The easiest way to hold the cotton ball is between your first two fingers. Then use your thumb and third finger to smooth the thread.

6 When you've managed to spin about 10 inches of thin thread (25 centimeters), wind the thread around the shaft of the whorl just above the wheel. Continue to wind the thread up the shaft until you've used up the cotton ball.

7 This might seem difficult at first, but if you keep practicing you'll quickly get the hang of it! If you want, once you have three or four pieces of yarn, you can dye them and braid them together to make a bracelet.

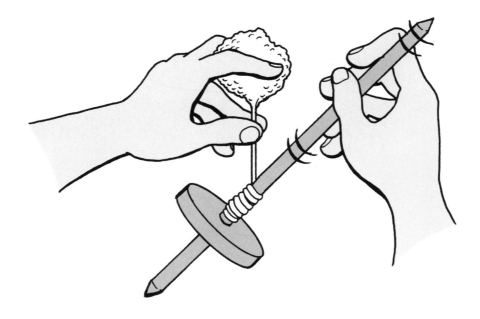

 51

MAYA CHILDREN

The birth of a child was the most important event in a Maya family. Childbirth was considered a sign of good fortune and a show of a family's wealth. Each day of the year had a specific name for both boys and girls. Most Maya children were named after the day they were born.

Starting around five years old, boys worked in the fields with their fathers and girls helped their mothers cook, clean, spin yarn, weave, and make pottery. When boys were around three years old, their mothers tied a white bead in their hair to show their **purity**. When boys reached **puberty**, around 14 years of age, the bead was removed by a shaman-priest in a ceremony called the Descent of the Gods.

The boy then moved into a house with other young boys until his father decided it was time for him to marry, around 19 years of age. Young men painted their bodies and faces black before marriage and red after.

WORDS TO KNOW

purity: innocence or freedom from guilt or evil.

puberty: when a child's body transitions into an adult body.

When Maya girls were small, their mothers tied a tiny red shell

Maya symbol for dog.

around their waists with a string. When they reached 12 years of age, the shell was removed. Girls were usually married by the time they were 14 years old. Until they were married, girls could not look men in the eye. If a girl met a man along a path, she stepped aside and turned her back until he passed.

DID YOU KNOW?

The Maya had dogs as pets just like we do. Their dogs were hairless, and could sweat through their skin. This is unusual for dogs, because most can only cool themselves by panting.

What Maya children did throughout the day depended on the status of their families. The children of royalty and upper society had more time to play, whereas the children of commoners, farmers, and builders had to help out with farming or chores. Archaeologists have found some ancient Maya children's toys, including a jaguar figure made of clay.

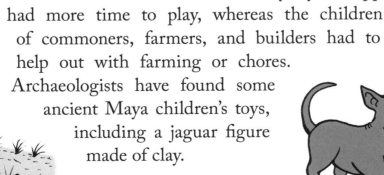

Beautiful Maya

The Maya idea of beauty was to look like the corn god. This meant they favored long heads and flowing hair. To change the shape of a newborn baby's head from round to long, they pressed the baby's soft skull between boards for a few days just after birth. They also tied wooden boards against the baby's forehead to flatten it and make it slope back. This changed the shape of the child's head forever. The Maya also considered crossed eyes beautiful. Parents would hang objects in front of a newborn's eyes until the baby's eyes were permanently crossed. Older children had their adult teeth filed to a point or a T-shape. Likely as a rite of passage into adulthood, holes were drilled into the front of their teeth and decorated with stones of jade, obsidian, or hematite. ⤷

An important family festival that is still celebrated today has roots in Maya history. According to legend, the spirits of the dead are brought to Mexico each year by the annual migration of monarch butterflies. The Day of the Dead is a traditional family holiday to celebrate and honor one's ancestors. People dress up like ghosts and skeletons. Families go to the cemetery where they clean and then decorate the graves of their ancestors with flowers and candles. At the cemetery there is a picnic with special food.

Atole is a traditional hot drink from Mesoamerica made from corn. In Mexico today, it is a common drink on the Day of the Dead.

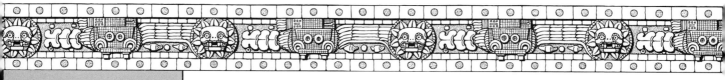

SUPPLIES

½ cup masa flour
(64 grams)

¼ cup hot water
(60 milliliters)

5 cups water
(about 1 liter)

blender

medium-sized saucepan

4 tablespoons chopped
piloncillo (unrefined
Mexican brown sugar)
or ¼ cup brown
sugar (about 55
grams) mixed with 2
teaspoons molasses

cinnamon

Make Your Own
MEXICAN *ATOLE*

See if you like this drink still prepared by Mexicans on the Day of the Dead today. *Ask an adult to supervise while you use the stove.*

1 Stir the masa flour and hot water together. Pour the water and the masa/water mixture into a blender, and blend until smooth. Then pour the mixture into the saucepan and warm on medium heat.

2 Once the mixture has thickened, add the *piloncillo* or brown sugar and molasses and stir until fully dissolved. Remove from the stove and pour into mugs. Sprinkle with cinnamon before serving.

Day of the Dead Today

Today, the Day of the Dead is most popular in Mexico, where it is a national holiday. It is a joyful celebration, honoring the lives of ancestors. According to today's version of the holiday, the souls of dead children return to Earth on November 1, and the adult spirits follow on November 2. Between October 31 and November 2, families clean the gravestones of their loved ones before loading them with sweets, food, and toys. Some families spend the night in graveyards, bringing pillows and blankets for their dead ancestors to rest in after their long journey from the underworld. Sugar cookies, sugar skulls, and *atole* are popular during this holiday. In some parts of the country, children in costumes roam the streets, asking for a *calaverita*, a small gift of money. ⟐

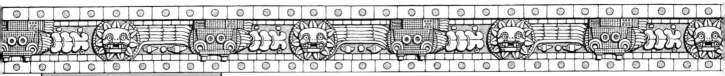

SUPPLIES

2 balloons (and some extras in case of pops!)

masking tape

2 toilet paper rolls cut in half or 1 paper towel roll cut into four pieces

microwave-safe mixing bowl

6 cups water (1½ liters)

3 cups flour (375 grams)

full sheets of newspaper

newspaper cut into thin strips

sewing needle or scissors

craft paint (black, brown, white)

paintbrush

spray varnish

2, quarter-inch dowels (½ centimeter)

4 wooden wheels with holes large enough for dowels to fit into

clay

Make Your Own
REPLICA OF A MAYA CHILD'S TOY

By making this homemade dog with wheels and giving it to a young child, you will see how Maya children enjoyed their pull-toys. *Ask an adult to supervise as you use a sharp sewing needle.*

1 Blow up one balloon to form the dog's body. Tie a knot in the neck of the balloon. Blow up a smaller balloon for the dog's head. Attach the smaller balloon to the larger one with masking tape.

2 Use the masking tape to attach the 4 pieces of cardboard rolls to the larger balloon. These will be the dog's legs.

3 Heat the water in the microwave. Mix the flour into the water until it makes a thick paste. Spread out some newspaper over your work surface. Dip strips of newspaper into the paste, but only as you need them or they will get soggy. Lay the newspaper strips all over the head and legs of the dog, until you've built up about four layers. This is very messy, but fun!

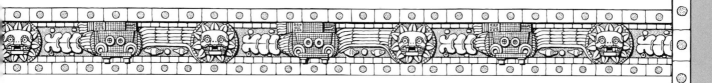

4 Set your dog aside and let it dry for a couple of days. You might want to place a cup or other support beneath the head of the dog as it dries so the head will not droop or fall.

5 When your dog is dry, burst the balloons with a sewing needle or a pair of scissors. Paint your dog white or brown (or spotted!). Use black paint to fill in features, such as ears, eyes, tail, and nose. Spray your dog with at least one coat of varnish to make it harder and to keep the paint from chipping.

6 Poke holes through opposite sides of the legs. Slide a dowel through each pair of legs and attach the wheels to the dowels.

7 Put a little ball of clay at each end of the dowels so the wheels don't come off.

Maya Wheels

Did the Maya know about the wheel? Experts think they did. The ancient Maya probably didn't use wheeled carts because the land was so rough and uneven. The carts would have to be pushed up hills, and probably would have gotten stuck in muddy and marshy areas. The Maya didn't have pack animals, such as donkeys and horses, so they would have had to pull the carts themselves. The only animal the Maya could have used to carry goods was the llama, but llamas are not sturdy enough to pull wheeled carts. Yet the Maya did put wheels on their children's toys!

GAMES

Every 20th day, the Maya held a religious festival to honor gods and goddesses. Ball games were an important part of the festivities. People from surrounding areas walked to the nearest city to watch the games.

Pok-A-Tok

One of the most well-known games the Maya played was a fast and furious ball game called Pok-A-Tok. Pok-A-Tok is believed to have been invented around 2000 BCE and played in every major Maya city.

Pok-A-Tok teams were usually made up of one to four players, who often worked in pairs. The object of the game was to get a ball through a narrow stone hoop that was located on the court wall, as high as 20 feet from the ground (6 meters). Players could not use their hands or feet—only their head, shoulders, elbows, wrists, and hips.

For the Maya, Pok-A-Tok was more than a game: it symbolized the struggle of life over death, and war and hunting. In general, only royalty were allowed to play and only priests could coach teams. Often, the losing team was sacrificed to the gods and the winners were given a feast. There is some belief that the winners were sacrificed, gaining direct entrance to heaven.

The sport was so difficult that games could last for days, ending when a player actually managed to get the ball through the ring on the wall.

The Maya sometimes played Pok-A-Tok just for fun. Players wore protective padding around their waists and on one shin and forearm because the game's hard, solid-rubber ball could seriously hurt or kill them. The balls were made of rubber from *cau-uchu* trees and were about as big as a basketball is today. The padding, called yokes, was made of cotton stuffed into wooden frames.

The largest ball court in Mesoamerica is at the ruins of Chichén Itzá, in Mexico's Yucatán peninsula. The Great Ballcourt of Chichén Itzá is 545 feet long and 225 feet wide (166 by 69 meters). The court walls are lined with carvings depicting the sacrifices made at the game's end. Next to the court is a stone platform decorated with hundreds of carved skulls—a visual reminder that many players lost their heads.

Bul

Some experts believe the ancient Maya played a game of chance called *bul*. In the Mayan language, the word *bul* means "dice." But *bul* was also a game of war: the goal of the game was to "kill" your opponent.

This game was played by adults and children, mostly by the wealthy, who had servants and more time for leisure activity. Though experts aren't exactly sure how the ancient Maya played the game, it is possible that they played it as the Maya living in Guatemala do today.

The Amazing Rubber Tree

Archaeologists have learned that many Mesoamerican people used rubber by 1600 BCE. Rubber was grown in the rainforest of the lowlands and then traded to surrounding areas. It wasn't just used for making balls. Rubber was used to attach stones to wooden handles, to seal bags that carried water, to waterproof clothing, and to make drumsticks for wooden drums. The Maya even coated their feet with layers of rubber to make a type of shoe. Rubber was also used by the shaman-priests to treat lip and ear wounds.

WORDS TO KNOW

latex: a milky fluid found in many plants.

To harvest rubber, the Maya made diagonal cuts in the bark of *cau-uchu* trees to drain the **latex** into their containers. Experts believe the rubber was combined with the juice of the morning glory vine to make a solid. This made the rubber tough, strong, and very elastic—perfect for bouncing. Before it hardened, which it did within minutes, the Maya were able to shape the rubber into whatever size ball they wanted. ༄

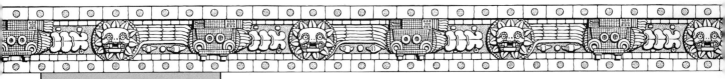

SUPPLIES

19 kernels of dried corn

flat playing surface
(floor or tabletop)

black magic marker

5 game pieces for
each player, like coins
or flat clay disks

PLAY BUL!

This is the version of *Bul* still played by the Maya in Guatemala today.

1 To start the game, you'll need to make your "game board." Simply place 15 kernels of corn in a straight line, each about 2 inches apart (5 centimeters), horizontally between you and your opponent. As you play, you will move your five game pieces in the spaces between the corn kernels.

2 Make your "dice" from four kernels of corn. Use the marker to draw a dot on one side of each kernel. When you throw the kernels, you get a point for every dot that faces up when the kernels land. If four blank sides face up, you get five points!

3 You also need to make your five game pieces. The ancient Maya may have used pieces of cotton, sticks, or stones. You can make yours from clay, but make sure each piece is about the same shape and size and that they can sit atop one another (for this reason flat disc shapes are ideal). If your game pieces are all the same color, paint one set a different color so you can tell yours apart from your opponent's.

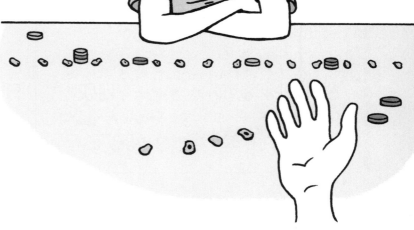

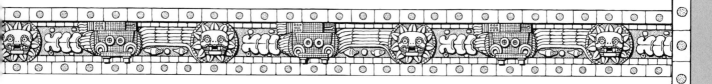

4 The game ends when one player loses all of his or her pieces. Here are the rules you need to know in order to play:

- Players place their game pieces at the end of the game board that is to their right. Players sit facing each other, so each moves along the board from their right to their left.

- The player to go first is the one who gets the highest number of points by throwing the four dice.

- The player to start throws the dice again, then moves a game piece the correct number of spaces. One point means a game piece moves one space to the left.

- The second player then throws the dice and enters the board from his or her end, so that the opposing game pieces are moving toward each other.

- On the second roll, players can either move the first game piece farther down the row or add a second game piece to the board.

- You cannot place two of your own pieces on the same space, but you can land on a space occupied by your opponent. When this happens, you can capture the piece by covering it with your piece. On the next throw, move the pieces together toward the end of the board.

- If you are able to get this game piece all the way to the end of the board without being landed on by your opponent, you get to keep your opponent's piece and put your piece back on the board by reentering it from the right side.

- The game gets really exciting if your opponent lands on a captured piece! When this happens, your opponent's piece sits atop the stack (which is now three levels high), and it now must be moved toward your opponent's end of the board (to his or her left). If your opponent is able to reach the end of the board without you intercepting the piece, his or her pieces can reenter the game board, and your piece is out of the game. How's that for reversal of fortune?

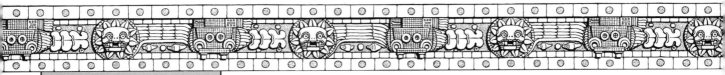

SUPPLIES

METHOD I:

aluminum foil

rubber bands

METHOD II:

jar of rubber cement

brush

Make Your Own
RUBBER BALL

This activity will show you two ways to make a rubber ball of your own. The first method is easier and faster. The second method is more authentic because it is all rubber, but requires more time and a ventilated area.

Method I:

1 Take a sheet of aluminum foil and crumple it into a ball. The foil ball can be any size, but the larger it is, the more rubber bands you'll need to cover it. You can also use just rubber bands by starting off with several rubber bands doubled up and wrapped around each other.

2 Stretch rubber bands over the foil one at a time until it's completely covered. Make sure you stretch the rubber bands completely around the ball so it stays as round as possible. Add each rubber band at a different angle so that your ball grows in an even way until it is the size you want.

Method II:

1 Spread a thin layer of rubber cement on a flat surface. Let it dry for a few minutes.

2 Start pushing your fingers around on the tacky rubber cement. It will peel off and gradually stick together. Roll it around to form a ball.

3 Spread another layer of rubber cement on your work surface. After it's dried for a few minutes, roll your ball around on the new layer. It will peel up and stick to your ball. Keep rolling it around and all the rubber cement will gradually form into a bigger ball.

4 Repeat this process as many times as you like, building up your rubber ball to the size you want.

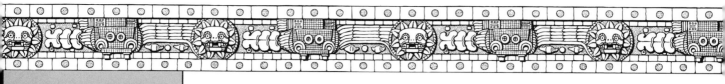

SUPPLIES

2 pieces of paper

pencil or pen

tape

a ball

Play a Version of
POK-A-TOK

The rules of this version of Pok-A-Tok are very simple, and you can play it yourself or with friends. Find a spot with two high walls that you can bounce a ball against.

1 Draw a circle 5 inches in diameter (13 centimeters) onto each piece of paper. If you are playing yourself you will only need one piece of paper and one wall.

2 Tape or tack the paper on opposite walls slightly above your head to start. While you can start the game at any height, remember that the higher the target, the more challenging the game will be.

3 If playing with a group, divide into two equal teams. Working together, try to hit the center of the circle on your team's target with the rubber ball without using your hands. The other team will try to take the ball away from you to hit their target, but they also cannot use their hands.

4 The first team to hit the target wins a point. When both teams have scored a point on their target, move the target higher. Or make the game more challenging by only using your feet, legs, and head. Imagine trying to play Pok-A-Tok like the Maya did, with a heavy rubber ball and a 20-foot-high ring (6 meters)—and remember the penalty for losing in ancient Maya culture was death!

  65

WRITING

One of the most impressive accomplishments of the Maya was their complex writing system. In fact, of the many societies that lived in Mesoamerica, only the Maya developed a complete system of written communication. This means that only the Maya could write down every syllable of their spoken language.

Hieroglyphics: Communicating through Pictures

The task of writing was given to scribes, who wrote in hieroglyphs, one of the world's most beautiful forms of writing. Hieroglyphs look like very detailed drawings of human and animal faces, circles, squares, and squiggly lines.

Maya symbol for book.

Scribes helped priests record their calculations and predictions. Another important job of the scribes was to record important events, such as wars and the birth of sons to the kings. As Maya writing took considerable skill and memory, scribes

WORDS TO KNOW

prominent: important.
distinctive: special or unique.
logogram: a written character that represents a meaning or word.

enjoyed a **prominent** position in society. Many scribes were members of the royal family, which allowed them to attend schools that taught them to write. Both male and female scribes wore a **distinctive** headdress, which announced to everyone who saw them that they were scribes. On Maya wall murals and pottery, scribes are shown with stick bundles in their headdresses. The stick bundles represented the tools of their trade: brush pens and quills.

DID YOU KNOW?

The ancient Mayan written language is a complex system of sounds, pictures, and **logograms**. Some of the hieroglyphs represent individual syllables, some are pictures that represent a word or idea, and some represent a spoken word or phrase.

WORDS TO KNOW

stucco: a durable finish for exterior walls, usually made of a mixture of cement, sand, limestone, and water, that is applied while wet.

Scribes used hieroglyphs to communicate numbers, dates, objects, titles, events, places, and names. They wrote on many types of surfaces, such as pottery, animal and human bones, and shells. They also carved glyphs into **stucco**, wood, and decorative stones such as jadeite. Hieroglyphs on palace and temple wall murals were considered so sacred that only the royals and priests were allowed to look at them.

• •

No matter where they left their mark, the scribes had two goals: to preserve the history of their kings and to make their kings look powerful.

• •

Experts have been studying Maya hieroglyphs since Stephens and Catherwood published *Incidents of Travel in Yucatán* in 1843. But it took more than 100 years for researchers to really understand the Mayan language. Scholars first discovered that some of the Maya symbols stood for periods of time. In 1958, a scholar by the name of Heinrich Berlin figured out that the glyphs identified specific places. Another scholar, Tatiana Proskouriakoff, was the first to prove that certain glyphs recorded the reigns of Maya kings. Finally, in 1973, experts succeeded in decoding the Mayan language. Today, experts know the meaning of 90 percent of their hieroglyphs.

Many of the hieroglyphs represent a single syllable. There are approximately 800 symbols! Scribes strung words and sentences together by writing out combinations of these symbols. The scribes usually wrote sentences in this format: distance number-date-verb-object-subject. The distance number is a date and tells the reader the number of days, weeks, months, and years that occurred between an event described in the prior sentence and an event being described in a current sentence.

One reason it took experts so long to understand the Mayan language is that so many glyphs stood for the same syllable. For example, there are at least five different glyphs a Maya scribe could choose for the syllable *ba*! Also, many of the hieroglyphs are logograms. So, while some scribes used multiple glyphs to spell out a word phonetically, syllable by syllable, other scribes used a single glyph to represent a complete word.

Some scribes, for example, chose to write the name of Pacal the Great using the "shield" glyph because "Pacal" translates to "shield." Other scribes chose to spell his name out phonetically as "pa-cal-la." This is similar to choosing whether to put six letters on a public restroom door to spell out "toilet" or drawing a simple stick figure of a man or woman on a restroom door.

Each scribe wrote the hieroglyphs in his or her unique style. It took the experts a long time to realize that hieroglyphs that looked similar were, in fact, the same.

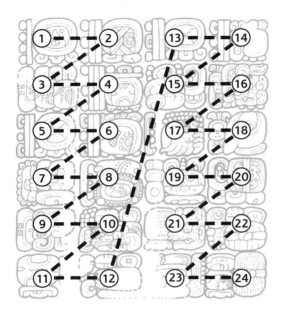

All scribes used the same format to present their information. They used paired columns stacked together to make sentences. The first glyph was on the top left, and the second was just to the right of the first. The third glyph was under the first, and the fourth was under the second. This continued in a zig-zag pattern all the way to the bottom of the column. The next paired column started back up at the top again.

When carving hieroglyphs into stelae, scribes first laid them out using ink. When they had the spacing right, they used wooden mallets and flint- or quartz-tipped tools to carve into the soft limestone.

Codices: Ancient Books

Although scribes wrote in many different places, they spent most of their time writing in special books made of paper called codices. Within these books, scribes faithfully recorded centuries of Maya history, astronomical calculations, religious practices, travel and hunting, and predictions of when an eclipse of the sun would occur.

Of the thousands of codices created, only four remain today. That's because during the Spanish conquest of the Maya, Spanish soldiers burned the codices.

WORDS TO KNOW

pagan: someone who worships many gods, or who has little or no religion.

horoscope: a prediction of a person's future based on the position of the planets and stars.

prophecy: a prediction of the future.

forgery: a copy, not the original.

The Spanish destroyed the **pagan** codices because they believed they were the work of the devil. Three of the codices have been found in European libraries. Experts believe they ended up in Europe when Spanish explorers sent them home as souvenirs. These codices are named after the cities where they are now located: Dresden, Germany; Madrid, Spain; and Paris, France.

The Dresden Codex discusses astronomy and includes tables for predicting solar eclipses. The Madrid Codex includes **horoscopes** and **prophecies**, and the Paris Codex highlights Maya rituals and ceremonies. A fourth codex, called the Grolier Codex, talks about how the planet Venus affected Maya religion and astrology. It was first displayed at the Grolier Club in New York City and may be a **forgery**. Though no one knows where it was discovered, the Grolier Codex is now housed in Mexico City, Mexico.

Why Did the Spanish Burn the Codices?

Diego de Landa (1524–1579), the Spanish priest in charge of converting the Maya to Christianity, ordered the burning of the Maya codices. Because many of the writings were records of Maya religious ceremonies, de Landa considered them to be non-Christian and therefore evil. He burned thousands of the codices in huge bonfires. In his journal, de Landa wrote that the Maya were deeply upset that he had destroyed their written history. De Landa had his Catholic priests torture and kill any Maya who resisted conversion to Christianity. The priests whipped the Maya for worshipping their gods, scalded them with boiling water, and even stretched their joints with ropes and pulleys. More than 5,000 Maya were tortured and more than 150 died. De Landa also ordered the Maya temples torn down. Some Spanish priests were so upset at de Landa's treatment of the Maya that they turned against Spain. ᔕᑎ

Scribes had to make their own paper from the bark of wild fig trees. First, scribes stripped the inner bark from the trees and boiled it in lime water to soften. After rinsing the bark in clean water, they pounded it with stone tools called *muinto* until it was very thin and wide.

They layered sheets of the flattened bark on top of each other, alternately laying them horizontally and vertically, so the tree fibers crossed each other and made the paper strong and thick enough to have writing on both sides. The paper was set to dry in the hot sun and then individual sheets were joined together, end to end, to make one long piece. The *muinto* made the beaten side of the paper rough, so scribes rubbed the paper with smooth, heated stones.

Scribes then used a wooden tool with a straight edge to crisply fold the paper back and forth on itself, like a fan or an accordion. The folded pages made it easy for scribes to open or close a book to the pages they wanted to see. But before they could write in the books, they needed to prepare the paper to absorb ink by painting both sides with a layer of gesso, a thin plaster made from ground white limestone and water.

When the gesso was dry, the pages were refolded and the books covered in protective binders made from wood and jaguar pelts. Experts believe the protective covers were detachable. The covers were probably placed on the codices when they were being read or written on, but removed when the codices were stored. This belief is backed up by the fact that none of the surviving codices has a cover, and archaeologists have unearthed many clay pots decorated with images of scribes writing in codices protected by covers made from jaguar pelts.

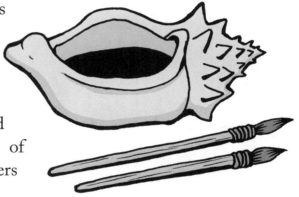

Just as the scribes used a grid when carving glyphs on other surfaces, they also used grid lines in their codices to plan the layout, as the books were too important to mess up.

As they worked, scribes used very thin brushes and quills to apply ink to the book pages. Their brushes were made from different thicknesses of animal hair. Conch shells, cut lengthwise, served as ink pots. Black ink was made from soot and red ink from a mineral called hematite. Because Maya scribes used mostly black and red inks, the Aztec named the Maya lowlands the Land of Black and Red.

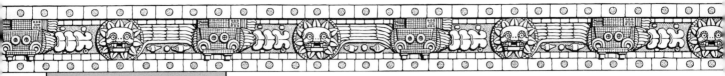

SUPPLIES

1 cup all-purpose flour (250 grams)

2 cups water (250 milliliters)

aluminum pan or any shallow dish

spoon

scissors

several sheets of unlined, white paper, any size

aluminum foil

rolling pin

marker

Make Your Own
PAPER

Try making your own woven homemade paper that you can actually write on. Have fun practicing some glyphs when you're done!

1 Mix the flour and the water in your pan. You can use the spoon, but your fingers will work just as well! Make sure you stir until there are no more clumps of flour. Set the pan aside.

2 Cut the paper into 1-inch-wide strips that are roughly the same length (2½ centimeters). Don't worry if some of the pieces are longer than others; you can trim them off later. Put the strips of paper in the flour and water mixture, and let them soak for several minutes. Make sure the pieces aren't sticking together. Move them around so each piece is covered in the mixture. While your paper soaks, spread out a piece of foil on a smooth, hard surface.

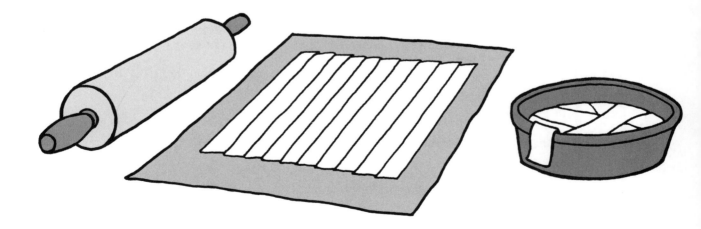

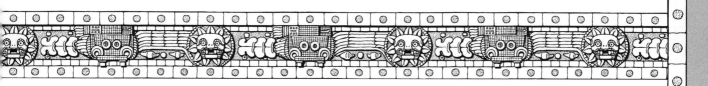

3 Carefully take the strips out, one at a time. Use your fingers to gently "squeegee" off the extra mixture. Lay half of the strips on the foil horizontally, making sure each piece slightly overlaps the one next to it. Lay the other half of the strips of paper vertically. When you are done, you should have two layers that are perpendicular to each other.

4 Lay a piece of foil on top of your paper strips. Firmly roll the rolling pin over the foil. Some of the flour and water mixture may seep out at the sides. After a few minutes of rolling, slowly pull back the top piece of foil. If some of the paper strips stick to it, gently pull them off and put them back down. (You don't need to roll them again.) Put your paper sheet, still on the bottom piece of foil, out in the sun to dry. Make sure it's on a flat surface. You can also leave it inside to dry, but it will just take a little longer.

5 When your paper is dry, carefully pull it away from the foil. Hold it up to the light. Notice the crisscross pattern? That's what the paper the Maya made looked like! Finally, trim the edges and use a marker to draw glyphs on it.

DID YOU KNOW?

The ancient Maya made their codices in varying lengths. When folded, the Dresden Codex is only 3½ inches wide (9 centimeters). But when its accordion-style pages are fully unfolded, it is nearly 12 feet long (over 3½ meters).

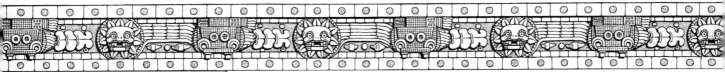

2 pieces letter-size white construction paper, or use the paper you made in the previous activity

ruler

pencil

scissors

clear Scotch tape

thin sheet of letter-size cardboard (the bottom of a writing pad works well)

black and brown markers or paint and paintbrush

ribbon

Make Your Own
CODEX REPLICA

Use the paper you made in the previous activity to complete your own codex.

1 Lay one sheet of the paper on the table lengthwise in front of you. Use your ruler to measure in 9 inches from the left margin of the paper (23 centimeters) and draw a vertical line. Cut along the line.

2 Use your ruler to measure 3 inches from the left edge (7½ centimeters), mark that spot with your pencil, then move your ruler 3 more inches to the right (7½ centimeters), and mark that spot. Your paper is now evenly divided into three 3-inch sections (7½ centimeters each).

3 Lay your ruler vertically on the first mark and carefully fold the paper over the left edge of the ruler. Move your ruler over to the next mark and fold the paper over again. You now have two hard creases. Refold the second crease in the opposite direction, under the sheet, so that the paper is folded like a fan.

4 Repeat these three steps for the second piece of paper. Connect the two pieces of paper using the Scotch tape. Make sure the folds alternate in an accordion before you tape the two ends together.

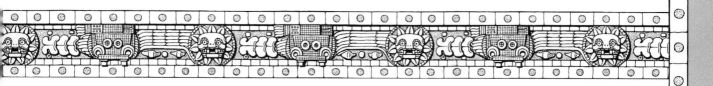

5 You now have a single codex book. Your top sheet should open on the right, just like a printed book. You can flip through the codex page by page or you can fully lay it out so that all six pages are visible at once.

6 To make the cover, place the cardboard on the table lengthwise in front of you. Use your ruler to measure in 6¼ inches from the left edge (16 centimeters) and draw a line. Cut along the line.

7 Fold the cardboard in half, so that you have a tall rectangle that is the same shape as your codex. Decorate the outside of the cover with your brown and black markers or paint it so that it looks like a jaguar pelt or leather.

8 When the cover is finished (make sure the paint is dry), slip the codex pages you made into the cover. You can tie a ribbon around it to keep it closed.

DID YOU KNOW?

Experts believe scribes made black ink for their codices by adding water to the soot scraped from the bottom of cooking pots. This soot is called carbon ink, and it is permanent. This is why epigraphers are still able to read the hieroglyphs of the Maya codices that survive today.

ACTIVITY

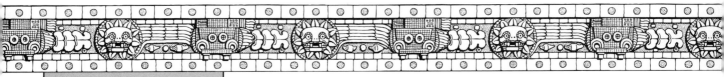

SUPPLIES

internet access

rounded bar of
bath soap

ballpoint pen

red and green
food coloring

cotton swabs

tissue

Make Your Own
SOAP GLYPH CARVING

In this activity, you're going to make your own mini-stela by carving the Maya hieroglyph for book, *hu'un*. When you're done, you can find the hieroglyphs for many more words by going to **famsi.org/mayawriting/ dictionary/montgomery/ search.html.**

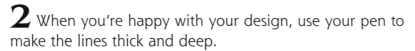

1 Using the hieroglyph symbol for "book" as your guide, use the ballpoint pen to lightly trace the design of the hieroglyph onto your bar of soap. As the hieroglyph is contained within a smooth-cornered square, the shape of your soap bar can represent the outside border of the hieroglyph.

2 When you're happy with your design, use your pen to make the lines thick and deep.

3 Put a few drops of food coloring onto the top of a cotton swab. Use red or green, or mix them to make black. Run the swab through the grooved lines, making sure the color gets deep into the grooves.

4 Use a tissue to wipe any excess coloring off the surface of the soap, leaving the color only in your carved lines.

5 Display the hieroglyph in your room—or use it during your next bath!

NUMBERS

All Maya people learned to count. Both their calendars and counting system were based on the number 20. Farmers used the counting system when planting and harvesting crops, merchants used it when buying and selling goods, and builders used it to take measurements and determine angles.

Maya numbers were made up of just three symbols. A shell indicated zero. A dot represented the number one. A bar represented the number five.

Here's how the Maya wrote numbers 0 through 19:

👁	•	••	•••	••••
0	**1**	**2**	**3**	**4**
—	•⁄—	••⁄—	•••⁄—	••••⁄—
5	**6**	**7**	**8**	**9**
═	•⁄═	••⁄═	•••⁄═	••••⁄═
10	**11**	**12**	**13**	**14**
☰	•⁄☰	••⁄☰	•••⁄☰	••••⁄☰
15	**16**	**17**	**18**	**19**

If the Maya wanted to add or multiply larger numbers, they used "steps" that represented a multiplication of 20. That means the number written on step two was 20 times more than the number on step one.

			•	**Step 4 = 8,000–159,999**
		•	👁	**Step 3 = 400–7,999**
	•	👁	👁	**Step 2 = 20–399**
•	👁	👁	👁	**Step 1 = 1–19**
1	**20** 20 x 1	**400** 20 x 20	**8,000** 20 x 400	

And the number written on step three was 20 times more than the number on step two and so on.

Numbers 1 through 19 were on the lowest step, numbers 20 through 399 were placed on the second step, numbers 400 through 7,999 were placed on the third step, and numbers 8,000 through 159,999 were placed on the fourth step. If the Maya wanted to count larger numbers, they just kept adding steps to get to the number they wanted—even up to the hundreds of millions!

When the Maya were adding numbers on different steps, they wrote them on top of each other. For example, to write the number 32, the Maya put two bars and two dots on the first step (12) and a dot on the second step (20 x 1).

32

When the Maya wrote the number 407, they used the third step. Zero is a place holder when there is no number needed on a step. They wrote a bar and two dots on the first step (7), a zero on the second step (0 x 20), and a dot on the third step (1 x 400).

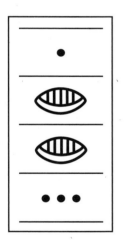

8,003

If the Maya wanted to write the number 8,003, they put three dots on the first step (3), a zero on the second step (0 x 20), a zero on the third step (0 x 400), and a dot on the fourth step (1 x 8,000).

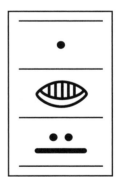

407

The Maya used names to signify the increased values of 20: *kal* (20), *bak* (20 x 20 = 400), *pic* (20 x 20 x 20 = 8,000), *calab* (20 x 20 x 20 x 20 = 160,000), *kinchil* (20^5 = 3,200,000), and *alau* (20^6 = 64,000,000).

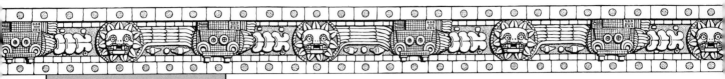

SUPPLIES

index cards

pencil or pen

clear packing tape
or contact paper

Make Your Own
MAYA COUNTING FLASH CARDS

These cards will help you learn to recognize Maya numbers quickly. You can use these cards to play games with friends or siblings.

1 Copy the Maya number symbols from page 80 onto 20 index cards. On the back of each card, write the number for that symbol.

2 "Laminate" the cards with a layer of the tape or contact paper on the front and back. This will keep the cards from getting dirty and crumpled.

3 Hold each card up to two friends and see who guesses the number first. You already know the answer because you've written it on the back of the card!

4 Once this game becomes too easy, try playing with two cards at the same time. Add to the challenge by making your friends add, subtract, or multiply the two numbers.

5 If you make two decks, you can play the game Concentration. Cover up the number on the back of the card with a small post-it sticker that's easy to remove. Place the 40 cards face down on the floor. When you correctly match two of the same card, you win the pair. Go again! The player with the most pairs at the end of the game wins. You can even use the cards to play a game of Go Fish or War.

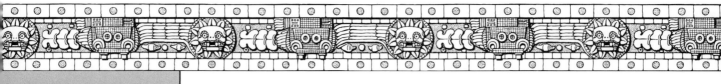

SUPPLIES

scrap paper

pencil or pen

Make Your Own
MAYA NUMBERS

Have you got the hang of it yet? Try this activity to test your Maya number knowledge.

1 See if you can figure out the value of these number glyphs. Write your answers on a piece of scrap paper. When you're satisfied with your answers check them against the answer key at the bottom of the page.

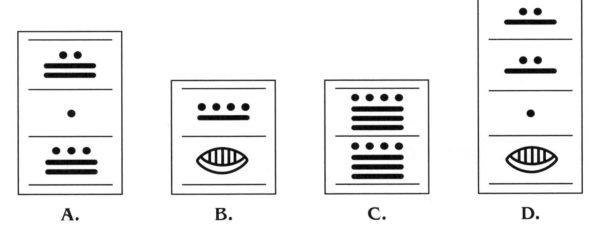

A.   **B.**   **C.**   **D.**

2 Now see if you can write your own number glyphs for the following numbers. Write your answers on a piece of scrap paper and check them against the answer key at the bottom of the page.

1,000	58	381	56,000
E.	**F.**	**G.**	**H.**

CHAPTER 10

TEN

CALENDARS

When archaeologists and other experts first began to study ancient Maya hieroglyphs, they were very confused, thinking the figures were gods. But then a German librarian named Ernst Forstemann figured out that some of the symbols stood for numbers. This knowledge helped experts figure out the Maya calendar. They quickly realized that the ancient Maya were obsessed with time. Maya calendars were the most complex in Mesoamerica and were more accurate than calendars being used in Europe at that time.

The ancient Maya relied primarily on two calendars for everyday life: the *tzolk'in* calendar, also called the **Sacred Round**, and the *haab*, also called the **Vague Year**. Both calendars were based on 20-day months. The Maya priests used the two calendars together to create a calendar of 52 years called the Calendar Round.

The *tzolk'in* was used to decide spiritual matters, such as when ceremonies should be held. The priests assigned each calendar day, called *k'in*, a god name and a number between 1 and 13. The first day of the *tzolk'in* calendar began with the number 1 and the first day name: 1 *Imix*. Turning the wheels in the direction of the arrows, the second day was 2 *Ik*. The 13th day was 13 *Ben*. But then the numbers ran out and started over. So, day 14 was 1 *Ix*. As the numbers cycled through the 20 names, it took 260 days for the *tzolk'in* calendar to start over at 1 *Imix*.

WORDS TO KNOW

tzolk'in or Sacred Round: a period of 260 days constituting a complete cycle of all the combinations of 20 day names with the numbers 1 to 13 that constitutes the Maya sacred year.

haab or Vague Year: the 365-day year of the Maya calendar.

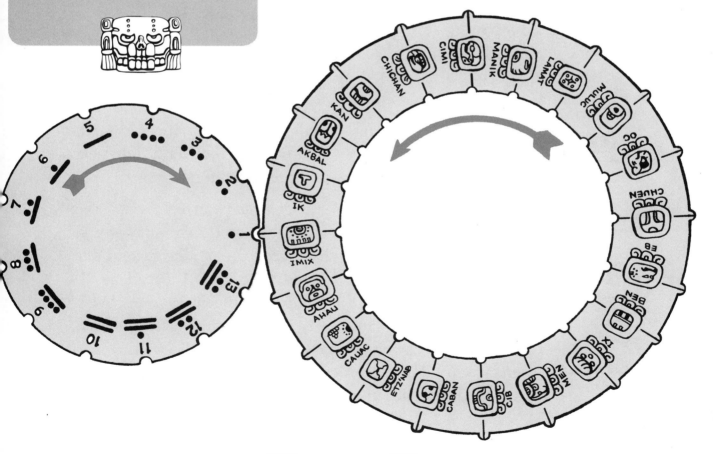

Pop (20 days)

Uo (20 days)

Zip (20 days)

Zotz (20 days)

Zec (20 days)

Xul (20 days)

Yaxkin (20 days)

Mol (20 days)

Ch'en (20 days)

Yax (20 days)

Zac (20 days)

Ceh (20 days)

Mac (20 days)

Kankin (20 days)

Muan (20 days)

Pax (20 days)

Kayab (20 days)

Cumku (20 days)

Uayeb (5 days)

The *haab* calendar was based on a 365-day solar cycle, the number of days in the calendar we use. The priests used the *haab* to decide when farmers should plant their crops. The *haab* had 18 months that were each 20 days long. The names of the 18 months were *Pop, Uo, Zip, Zotz, Zec, Xul, Yaxkin, Mol, Ch'en, Yax, Zac, Ceh, Mac, Kankin, Muan, Pax, Kayab,* and *Cumku.*

But 18 months multiplied by 20 days is only 360 days. The Maya added five unlucky days, together called *Uayeb*, to the end of the calendar. On these unlucky days, when it was believed that gods rested and left the earth unprotected, the Maya didn't eat and they offered many sacrifices.

The *haab* started with the number 0, so the first day would have been 0 *Pop*. The second day would have been 1 *Pop*. Day 20 would have been 19 *Pop*. With that, all of the 20 days in the *Pop* month would have been used up, so the next day would start with the month *Uo*. The *haab* calendar started over after cycling through each day of the 18 months and then five unlucky days.

When the priests used the *tzolk'in* and the *haab* calendars together as the Calendar Round, they could see 18,980 days (52 years) at one time. In the Calendar Round, the two calendars rotated together, like cogged wheels, and the dates from each calendar were combined. The first day of the Calendar Round was 1 *Imix* 0 *Pop*. As the Calendar Round had to cycle through all 18,980 days, it took 52 years for 1 *Imix* 0 *Pop* to line up again. The Maya referred to these 52-year periods as "bundles," much like we call 100-year periods "centuries." At the end of the 52-year cycle, there was a sacred day. The Maya feared this day, as they believed the sky would fall on them if the gods were unhappy with humans.

A third Maya calendar, called the **Long Count**, was used only by Maya priests and scribes because it was so challenging to understand. They used this calendar to record long periods of time—even from the start of creation.

The calendar began on August 13, 3114 BCE. One complete cycle of the Long Count was designed to last around 1,872,000 days. The end of this Great Cycle lands on December 21, 2012. It will be a winter solstice when the sun will be in the center of our galaxy (the Milky Way) for the first time in over 26,000 years! On December 21, 2012, the calendar does not end, but will go to the next *bak'tun*, or 400-year period (the 13th).

The Long Count was primarily based on the number 20. The Maya wrote the dates in this order: *bak'tun, k'atun, tun, uinal, k'in*. 1 *k'in* = 1 day, 20 *k'ins* = 1 *uinal* (month), 18 *winals* = 1 *tun* (360 days), 20 *tuns* = 1 *k'atun* (7,200 days), 20 *ka'tuns* = 1 *bak'tun* (144,000 days or 400 years).

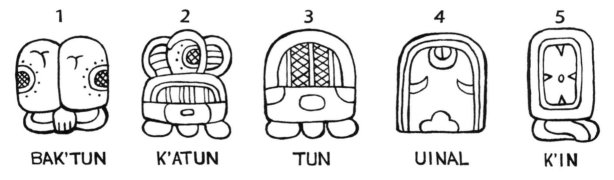

1	2	3	4	5
BAK'TUN	K'ATUN	TUN	UINAL	K'IN

If we look at December 21, 2012, it would be written as 12.19.19.17.19. The number 12 represents the number of *bak'tuns* since the beginning of the Great Cycle (144,000 x 12), continuing to the right with the number of *k'atuns, tuns, uinals,* and *k'ins*.

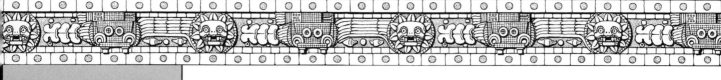

SUPPLIES

letter-size sheet of heavy white cardstock

mathematical compass

glyphs chart (page 85)

tracing paper

pen or pencil

scissors

glue stick

Make Your Own
TZOLK'IN CALENDAR WHEEL

The Maya calendar is complex and the best way to really understand it is to make your own. After you practice for a while, see if you can start to predict the next day without looking at the calendar.

1 Use your mathematical compass to draw two circles on your piece of cardstock: one with a diameter of 6 inches (15 centimeters) and the other with a diameter of 4 inches (10 centimeters). Cut out both circles.

2 Trace each of the *tzolk'in* calendar glyphs from the picture on page 85. Cut each one out and glue them along the outer edge of the large circle, in the right order, making sure they're evenly spaced and facing in the same direction.

3 Write the glyphs for the numbers 1 through 13 evenly spaced along the edge of the small circle.

4 Lay the two circles next to each other on your table. Line the number 1 up with the first month, *Imix*. Turn the number circle clockwise and the day circle counter clockwise, so that you see that day two is 2 *Ik*, day three is 3 *Ak'bal* . . . and day 13 is 13 *Ben*. What is the date of the 14th day? Yes! It's 1 *Ix*, because the numbers start over. But what's the 27th day? And the 40th? And the 53rd?

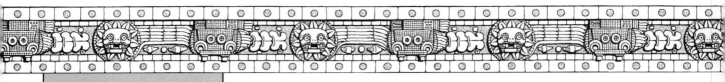

Figure Out Your Own
MAYA DATES

Try working with the *tzolk'in* and *haab* to see how truly complicated Maya calendars were. Imagine adding in the Long Count and you'll understand why only priests and scribes used it!

8 *Ben* 14 *Pax*
(day 8 *Ben* of the *tzolk'in* and 6th *Pax* month of the *haab*)

1 Using the *tzolk'in* and *haab* glyphs included in this section and the example above, try drawing the glyphs for these Calendar Round dates:

13 *Ix* 3 *Cumku*
(day 13 *Ix* of the *tzolk'in* and 3rd *Cumku* month of the *haab*)

A.

2 *Cauac* 4 *Zip*
(day 2 *Cauac* of the *tzolk'in* and 4th *Zip* month of the *haab*)

B.

1 *Ik* 19 *Pop*
(day 1 *Ik* of the *tzolk'in* and 8th *Pop* month of the *haab*)

C.

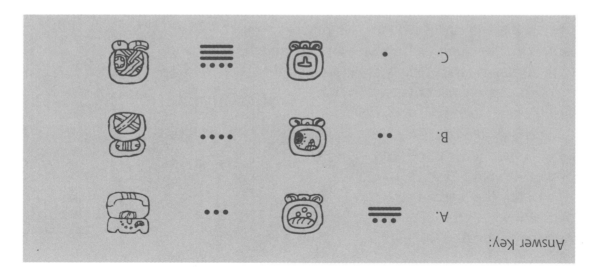

Answer key:

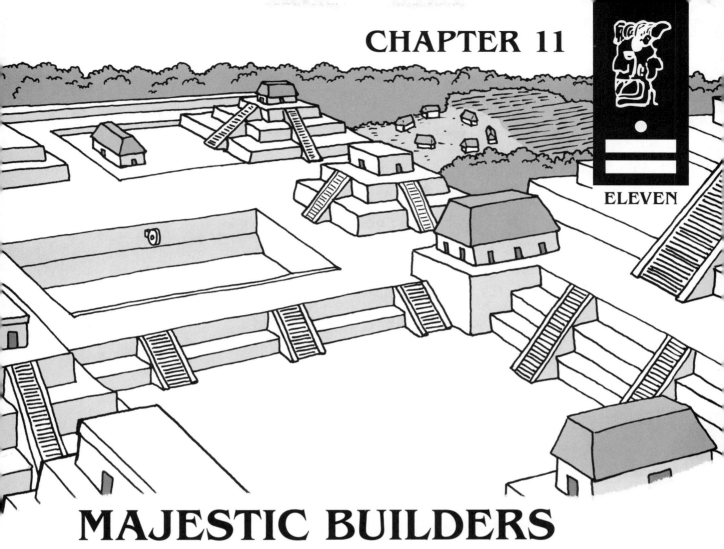

MAJESTIC BUILDERS

By their classic period (250–900 CE), the ancient Maya had built impressive cities and miles of the best roadways in Mesoamerica. Some of their roads have survived to this day.

Maya engineers and **laborers** even considered how the rainy season would affect the roads because they didn't want them to get washed away. In swampy areas, roads were built high above the ground to protect them from flooding.

The ancient Maya were careful to build their roads level. They may have used a **plumb bob**, a simple tool they used in building their pyramids. The plumb bob is one of the oldest building tools in the world. It is easily made by hanging a heavy weight from a cord. When the plumb bob hung straight, the Maya knew they had a perfect vertical line.

In the city squares, Maya laborers built tall pyramids topped with temples and sacrificial altars. Workers also built Pok-A-Tok ball courts, bathhouses, and buildings used to conduct official city business. Laborers built observatories where priests could study the night skies and stone palaces and homes for members of the large royal families.

WORDS TO KNOW

laborer: someone who works with his or her hands.

plumb bob: a weight on the end of a line, used especially by builders to establish exact vertical and horizontal lines.

plentiful: available in large amounts.

quarry: to dig or cut rock from the earth.

The ancient Maya used limestone for most of their important city buildings, as it was strong and **plentiful**. Workers **quarried** large blocks of limestone from the ground using chisels with sharp flint and obsidian blades. How could these tools cut through stone so easily? Limestone is actually soft when buried underground, and only hardens when it is dug up and exposed to the air.

After cutting the limestone from the **bedrock**, Maya laborers pried the blocks loose using wooden mallets and wedges. They then had to take the blocks back to their cities. They pulled the blocks across the ground with rope, or rolled them along the tops of logs, or sometimes they floated the blocks down the rivers on rafts.

Buildings were constructed from the limestone blocks, held together with quick-drying **mortar**. The mortar was made by putting smaller pieces of limestone or large amounts of shells into big bonfires. The heat of the fire reduced the stone or shells to a fine powder, which was then mixed with gravel and water to make the mortar.

The mortar could be thinned out with a bit more water to make stucco, which was applied to walls, stairways, and doorways. Because stucco was softer than mortar, the workers who specialized in carving could easily decorate the buildings with religious designs and glyph symbols. Maya carvers didn't waste time or effort in their work: if only one side of a building was seen during religious ceremonies, then only that side was decorated. When the carvings were finished, laborers painted the walls a bright red, which made them stand out from the green of the trees and the blue of the sky. The paint wore off many, many years ago, which is why Maya ruins look gray today.

Workers who specialized in carving were called *ah uxul*. They often worked in groups on building projects or when carving symbols into the stelae. Experts know this because some stelae have group signatures.

A thick layer of stucco was also used to protect buildings from the humidity of the rainforests by sealing the buildings against rain. Builders in the cities used stone rubble to build the foundations of their buildings because limestone is too soft to hold up against years of heavy rains and flooding.

Carvers also used stucco to add decoration to the roof combs they built atop important buildings. Roof combs are blocks of stone added to building roofs to make the structures appear taller than they actually are. In some Maya cities, such as Tikal, roof combs are often taller than the buildings they sit on! To support their great weight, the Maya built roof combs over the thickest walls of the buildings.

Burial

Some pyramids contained the burial tombs of important Maya kings such as Pacal II, also known as Pacal the Great, who ruled the great city of Palenque. Standing about 100 feet tall (30 meters), Pacal's burial pyramid is called the Temple of Inscriptions. When Pacal the Great died in 683 CE, his body was carried up the pyramid's outer steps and down an 80-foot interior stairway that led to his crypt (24 meters). Five victims were sacrificed outside the door of his tomb. Workers then sealed off the tomb by filling the stairway with stone rubble.

King Pacal's tomb remained sealed until 1948, when a Mexican archaeologist named Alberto Ruz Lhuillier discovered the secret stairway. It took his team four years to remove all the rubble the ancient Maya laborers had carted in to protect Pacal II's heavily jeweled corpse. They finally opened the doorway to the tomb in 1952, finding the king's skeleton and jade jewels!

The **corbel arch** was used a lot by Maya builders. In addition to being used to reduce the weight of roof combs, it was used in buildings to create doorways, corridors, and peaked rooms. The corbel arch is a perfect example of the technical skill of the ancient Maya. Not only did the engineers and builders have to understand the stress the stone blocks put on each other, they had to figure out how wide, high, and thick to make each block. They even had to factor in the amount of space the mortar took up between each stone block.

WORDS TO KNOW

corbel arch: an arch shaped like an upside-down V that is formed by a series of overlapping stones with each stone jutting out farther toward the center than the one below it. The space left at the end is bridged by a **capstone**.

capstone: the final, topmost stone in a corbel arch, which joins the sides and completes the structure.

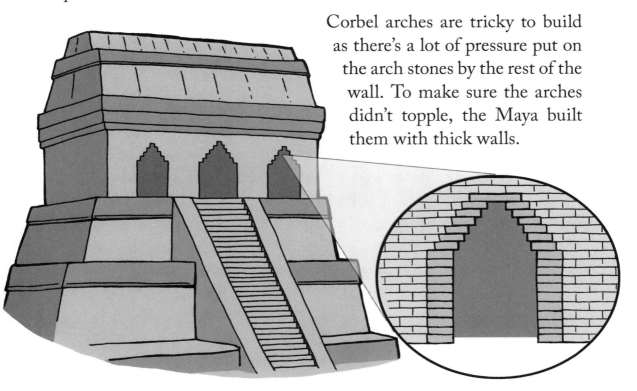

Corbel arches are tricky to build as there's a lot of pressure put on the arch stones by the rest of the wall. To make sure the arches didn't topple, the Maya built them with thick walls.

Watch the Spirit Snake Slither!

The most famous example of a Maya building with sacred "power" is a pyramid at the ruins of Chichén Itzá, a large city-state. At the top of this pyramid is a temple called El Castillo, the Spanish term for "the Castle."

The temple of El Castillo was dedicated to Kukulkán, the Feathered Serpent god. Kukulkán is known as Quetzalcoatl to the Olmec and Aztec. Each staircase faces a direction on a compass. There are staircases leading up the four sides of the pyramid. If you add up the 91 steps of each staircase, you get the number 364, and if you add the flat platform at the top of the pyramid, you get 365—the number of days in the *haab*, the Maya solar calendar. Each side of the pyramid has 52 rectangular panels, which is equal to the number of years of one complete "bundle," or cycle, of the Calendar Round.

At the vernal and autumnal equinoxes each year (around March 21 and September 22), thousands of tourists gather on the northwest side of El Castillo. During the equinox, day and night are about the same length all around the world. On these days, as the sun gradually illuminates the stairs of El Castillo, spectators are treated to a solar phenomenon: it appears that a shadow snake is slithering down the steps from the heavens to Earth!

Ancient Maya engineers designed buildings to be impressive on the outside. They cared much less about what they looked like or how comfortable the buildings were on the inside. Some experts believe the Maya built for one reason only: to create lavish stages for their city-wide ceremonies when human sacrifices were made to the gods. The eyes of thousands of city residents were glued to the kings and priests as they climbed the steep pyramid steps to the sacred sacrificial altars. Imagine how impressive this sight must have been amid the blaring horns, pounding drums, and people shouting!

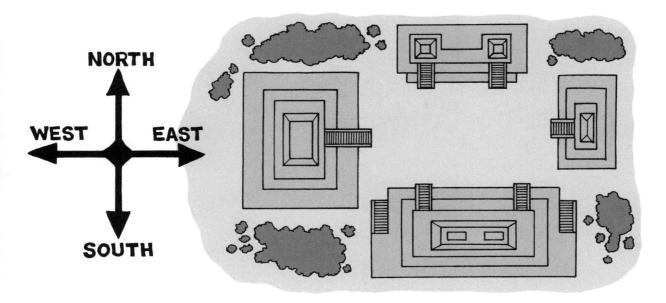

The ancient Maya aligned their ceremonial buildings with the points of the compass to make sure the gods saw their cities as sacred places. As cities grew larger, new buildings were added in proper alignment to the stars.

Trees, Trees, and More Trees!

Though the ancient Maya built their important city structures out of stone, as a society they were very dependent on trees. Wood from trees fueled fires, which were necessary to cook food, keep warm, and make limestone powder or mortar. Without trees, the Maya would have been unable to make their canoes, the handles for tools, many of their musical instruments, and paper for the codices! Without trees, many of the birds and animals who relied on their seeds and foliage for food and shelter would have died. Without cacao trees, Maya kings would not have had access to cacao beans for their favorite chocolate drink. And without trees to hold the soil in place, much of the land would have washed away with the rains during the long rainy season.

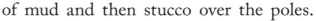

While workers built massive temples for their kings, they built simple homes of mud and thatch for themselves, and covered them with stucco for protection during the rainy season. It is unclear why the commoners didn't live in stone houses, but it probably had to do with cost and the fact that wealthy and important members of Maya society kept the limestone for themselves.

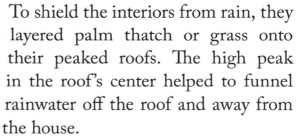

Mud homes were certainly easier to build than stone houses. To build a mud home, the Maya packed down a raised platform of dirt with their feet. A retaining wall of stones held the raised platform in place. The laborers then used wooden poles to make the walls and the peaked roofs of their houses. They added layers of mud and then stucco over the poles.

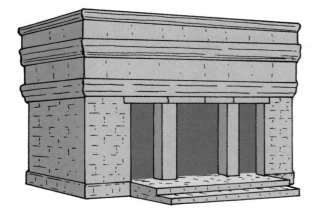

To shield the interiors from rain, they layered palm thatch or grass onto their peaked roofs. The high peak in the roof's center helped to funnel rainwater off the roof and away from the house.

The nobles had the better stone homes. The stone kept their houses warm when it was cold outside and cool during the midday heat. And, as stone doesn't burn, the nobles didn't have to worry about kitchen fires as much as the commoners did. And then there's the pest issue: insects really like wood and grass! Because commoners had more bugs in their homes, they probably got sick more often than nobles did.

  98

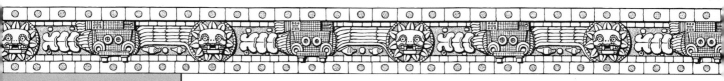

SUPPLIES

large piece of thick cardboard, such as the lid of a pizza box

pencil

colored paper

scissors

fine-tip black marker

toothpicks

Elmer's glue

mixing bowl

2 cups all-purpose flour (250 grams)

1 cup table salt (250 grams)

1 tablespoon lemon juice

1 cup water (250 milliliters)

plastic spoon

decorations such as beads, feathers, and glitter

craft paints (blue and at least three other colors)

paint brush

Make Your Own
RUIN MAP OF THE MAYA HOMELAND

This project will give you a clear understanding of where you can travel today to visit ancient Maya ruins.

1 On your piece of cardboard, draw the outline of the ancient Maya homeland using the image on the next page as a guide. Be sure to leave room for the Pacific Ocean, the Caribbean Sea, and the Gulf of Mexico. Set this map aside.

2 Cut five small diamonds out of your colored paper. Fold them in half to make triangle-shaped flags. Use your marker to label both sides of each flag with the names Chichén Itzá, Tikal, Palenque, Tulum, and Copán. Glue these flags around the toothpicks.

3 In a mixing bowl, combine the flour, salt, and lemon juice. Slowly add water to create your salt dough. If the dough is too dry, add more water. If it is too sticky, add a bit more flour.

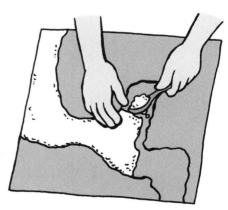

4 Use your spoon to carefully fill in all of the land area on your map, but leave the water areas uncovered.

Activity continued on next page . . .

5 While the dough is still wet, use a toothpick to carve the borders that separate modern-day Mexico, Guatemala, Belize, Honduras, and El Salvador. You can decorate the borders with beads or glitter.

6 Cut out five small rectangles of paper and write the name of one country on each. Use your finger to press the strips of paper into the dough on the appropriate areas of your map. Use your imagination to make the names stand out and look interesting.

7 Stick the toothpicks with the ruin names into the map where they belong. You can cut the toothpicks in half if you want the flags to be shorter.

8 Set your map aside for several days, until the dough has dried and hardened. The thicker your "land," the longer it will take to dry.

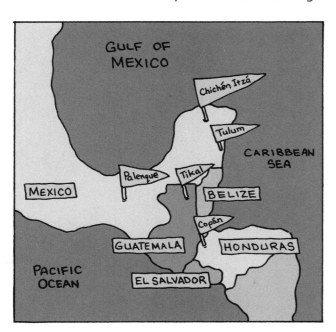

9 Once the dough is hard, paint the countries different colors. Use blue to color in the Pacific Ocean, Caribbean Sea, and Gulf of Mexico. Let the paint dry. Label these bodies of water with your marker.

10 To seal the dough so that your map will last longer, mix 1 tablespoon of Elmer's glue with 1 tablespoon of water. Use a paint brush to paint this mixture all over the salt dough to keep it from absorbing moisture.

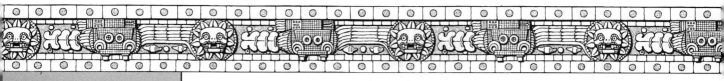

SUPPLIES

ruler

pencil

piece of paper

scissors

5 sheets of thin
cardboard such as
the backs of old
pads of paper

masking tape

glue

paintbrush

newspaper

red sand

Make Your Own
MODEL OF A MAYA PYRAMID

Look at pictures of the Egyptian pyramids and note how they were different from Maya pyramids. Build your own Maya pyramid and you'll understand why. Remember, Maya built their pyramids for religious purposes. Egyptian pyramids were built as burial tombs for their kings.

1 Use your ruler and pencil to draw an equilateral (all sides equal) triangle on your piece of paper. Make the sides at least 10 inches long (25 centimeters).

2 Cut out your triangle pattern and trace its shape onto each of four pieces of cardboard. Cut out each cardboard triangle, then stack them on top of each other. These will be the sides of your pyramid.

3 Draw a line about 4 inches from the top of each triangle, and cut off the top of each triangle at the same height (10 centimeters). Remember, the Maya built temples with flat tops! Set aside the snipped-off pieces—you'll need these to make the temple at the top of the pyramid.

4 Tape the four sides together as shown. Turn over the taped sides, fold them at the hinges, and stand it up. The tape should be on the inside. Seal the open side by taping it on the inside.

101

**Activity continued
on next page . . .**

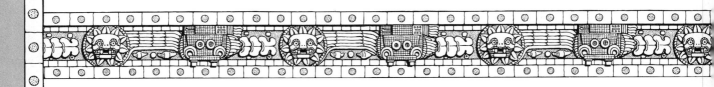

5 From a scrap of one of the pieces of cardboard, cut a square big enough to cover the hole at the top of your pyramid. Glue this to the top of your pyramid to make the base of your temple.

6 Take the four small triangles you set aside and stack them. Draw a line across the top and cut off the tops. To make your temple, cut a small rectangle for a door in one of the triangles. Tape these pieces together the same way you taped together the larger pieces. Cut another square from scrap cardboard to cover the top of your temple.

7 Use your paintbrush to spread glue on the bottom of your smaller cardboard square. Place it atop the temple and allow the glue to set for a few minutes. Then spread glue on the bottom of you temple walls and place it atop the pyramid.

8 Cut four strips of paper about 1 inch wide and 8 inches long (2½ by 20 centimeters). Fold each like an accordion for steps. Attach each with glue to the center of a pyramid side. Allow the glue to set.

9 Cover your work surface with the newspaper, and then spread a thin coat of glue on one side of the pyramid and steps. Sprinkle red sand on top of the glue. Do this with the other three sides and the top. This will give the pyramid its distinctive red Maya appearance.

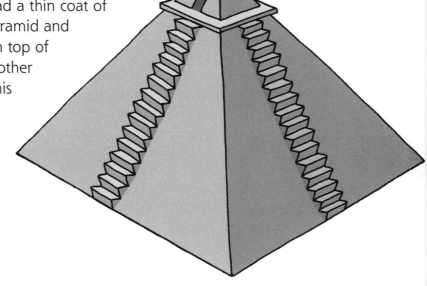

THE ARTS

The art of the Maya flourished during the classic period because Maya kings liked to be surrounded by beautiful things that showed the wealth of their cities.

Paintings

Artists painted vibrant scenes of royal life on temple walls. Maya art focused on the themes of blood sacrifices, war, and the deeds of great Maya rulers. The ancient Maya did not think it was important to show happy families playing with their children, or laborers building great pyramids. Instead, art depicted special ceremonies, such as kings and queens cutting their bodies to offer their blood to the gods. Artists also liked to show war captives being presented to victorious kings.

Carvings

As the most important people in their cities, kings wanted to see their lives recorded in stelae carvings. This was the primary way that kings displayed their power and accomplishments. Kings were always the central figures in the limestone and sandstone carvings, though they were often surrounded in the carvings by other people. Most artists carved figures in profile, facing left, and most ancient Maya carvings tend to look flat, rather than three-dimensional.

The magnificent clothing of kings, priests, and other nobles is clearly visible in Maya carvings. Very few pieces of actual clothing survive today because Central America is so humid that fabrics deteriorate quickly. Archaeologists have discovered, mostly from art on wall **frescos** and pottery, that for special ceremonies, weavers produced elaborate costumes for kings, priests, and nobles, sometimes with pearls and feathers woven right into the material.

WORDS TO KNOW

fresco: a work of art painted with pigment on wet plaster on a wall or ceiling.

During special ceremonies, kings wore headdresses decorated with jadeite, turquoise, and bird feathers, and cloaks made from spotted jaguar pelts. The spotted pelts were prized by priests and kings because they believed the spots represented the stars and that jaguars helped them to communicate with the spirit world. Maya kings also believed that jaguars protected royal families.

Jewelry

The royals wore a lot of jewelry, including bracelets, nose and ear plugs, earrings, knee bands, anklets, necklaces, bracelets, rings, and pendants. Jewelry was made from shark and crocodile teeth, as wells as claws, shells, obsidian, bone, wood, polished stone, and jadeite. Ear plugs are earrings that fit inside large holes cut into the earlobe. Common people wore simple nose plugs, lip plugs, and earrings of bone, wood, shell, and stone.

Maya royalty prized jadeite because its green color reminded them of fields of green corn stalks.

Mesoamerican jade, from the highlands of what is now Guatemala, is called "jadeite." Though green like the jade of China, it can also be black. Jadeite is a very hard stone that ranges in color from blue-green to nearly black.

DID YOU KNOW?

The Maya did not use gold or copper in their decorative items until their post-classic period (900–1524 CE), when they began accepting it in trade from the Aztec.

Because they prized it so much, Maya nobles even drilled
holes in their teeth and filled them with jadeite!

The Maya collected jadeite from the riverbeds of what is now Guatemala. Because jadeite is so hard, it takes great skill to carve. Flint, which the Maya used for cutting and carving limestone, was useless against jadeite. But the ancient Maya were able to saw jadeite into flat slabs by pulling a cord embedded with quartz pieces back and forth over its surface with the help of water and sand. They used bone drills to make decorative cuts and plant fibers to polish the surface of the stone.

Pottery

Maya produced world-class pottery using clay from the riverbeds. They strengthened the clay by adding calcite, quartz, or volcanic ash. Potters made clay pots for cooking, storing food, and for religious and medical purposes.

Maya potters used clay coils to build their pots. After building the coils up as high as they wanted, they smoothed the coils together with their fingers. They also used clay slabs to make ceramic boxes. Potters may have used an early potter's wheel called a *k'abal*, which is a wooden platform that they rotated. It allowed them to work on all sides of a piece without having to lift up the pot or change their sitting position.

To bake their unglazed pieces, Maya potters used low-temperature ovens heated by wood fires. These were often pits in the ground. To decorate the pottery with scenes of court life, they used paint made from a mixture of finely ground pigment, clay, and water. The heat of the ovens would have destroyed other dyes the potters could have used, so they used just a few colors that could stand up to the heat. These included black made from manganese, yellows and browns made from limonite, and oranges and reds made from hematite.

Potters usually outlined figures of animals and people in black, and used the yellows, browns, reds, and oranges to fill the figures in. The artists who painted the pottery made their paint brushes by attaching animal hair bristles or yucca fibers to a hollow tube. To give their pieces a high gloss finish, experts believe Maya artists rubbed the pieces with a resin.

The Powerful Jaguar

Jaguars look a lot like leopards, but their fur has larger black-rimmed spots called rosettes. The Central American rainforests offer jaguars plenty of cover as they stalk their prey. Jaguars have the strongest jaw of any cat found on the planet. Because of their power, many Maya kings added "Jaguar" to their name, including the Yaxchilán kings Shield Jaguar and Bird Jaguar.

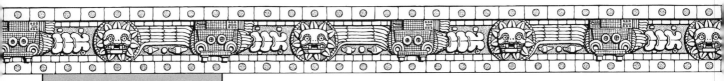

SUPPLIES

wax paper

masking tape

air-hardening clay OR
paperclay (available
in craft stores)

plastic knife or art tool

rolling pin

round cookie cutter

small bowl of water

toothpick (optional)

acrylic paints (optional)

Make Your Own
CLAY CUP

**Once you see how easy these are to make, you can
experiment with designs and try etching in some glyphs.**

1 Create an easy-to-clean work surface by taping a piece
of wax paper to a table or countertop.

2 Make the cup's base by cutting a chunk of clay and
rolling it out flat with a rolling pin. Cut out a round circle
using your cookie cutter.

3 Form a long coil by rolling a piece of clay between
your palms. Keep the coil the same thickness along its
length, so that your finished cup is even.

4 Place the coil along the outer edge of the round base. Use additional coils to build
up the sides of the cup until it is 3 or 4 inches high (about 8 to 10 centimeters).

5 When your sides are high enough, you
can dip your fingers into your bowl of
water and use the liquid to smooth the
coils together. Or you can keep the coil
look if you like its texture.

6 Use the toothpick to draw diamond
patterns into the surface of the cup. Let
your cup air dry.

7 If you want, you can use acrylic paints
to decorate the outside of the cup with
glyphs or color in the pattern.

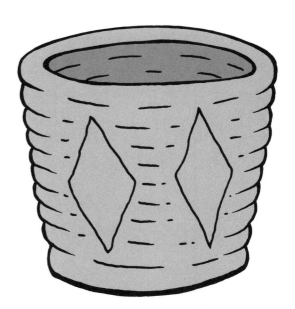

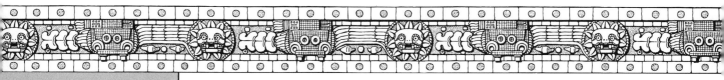

SUPPLIES

square piece of
light brown fabric
approximately 1 yard by
1 yard (about 4 square
meters)—flannel works
well because it doesn't
need to be hemmed

ruler

pencil

scissors

two 6-inch lengths
of brown ribbon
(15 centimeters)

needle and thread
OR stapler

picture of a jaguar

black felt (enough
to cover the cape
with jaguar spots)

hot glue gun or
fabric glue

Make Your Own
ROYAL JAGUAR CAPE

See how powerful you feel when you wear the cape of this sacred Maya symbol. *If you use a hot glue gun, ask an adult to supervise.*

1 Lay the fabric on a table in front of you. Take the bottom edge and fold it up to the top edge so that you've made a rectangle. Take the left edge and fold it over to the right edge so that you once again have a square, only smaller.

2 The bottom left corner is the center of your piece of fabric. This is where you'll cut your neck hole. Use your pencil to draw a curved line about 2 inches out from the corner's point (5 centimeters). Cut along this line.

3 To make your cape's rounded shape, draw another curved line, this time from the top left corner of your square down to the bottom right corner. Cut this rounded line. This line becomes the bottom edge of your cape.

4 You've now got a poncho shape. But let's cut the cape so that it's open. Unfold the top fold of your cape once so that your cape has the shape of a full rainbow. Your neck hole is at the bottom and the rounded hem edge is at the top. Cut the fold that is to the left of the neck hole, along the bottom edge. Now open the cape. Sew or staple the ribbon to the neck to make ties.

5 Study the photo of the jaguar, then cut similar shapes from your black felt and glue them to your cape. Use as few or as many spots as you like.

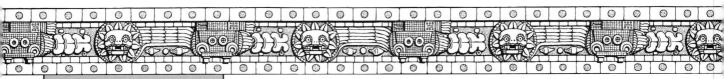

SUPPLIES

newspaper

wax paper or 8-by-10-inch glazed ceramic tile (20 by 15 centimeters)

elastic thread (green or white)

scissors

masking tape

Sculpey clay (green, black, white)

plastic knife or clay modeling tool

rolling pin

toothpicks (the heavy round kind)

index cards

thin wooden skewers

disposable foil trays

oven

Make Your Own
REPLICA OF A ROYAL MAYA JADEITE NECKLACE

In this activity, you'll make a replica of a jadeite burial necklace found in a royal tomb at Calakmul, a Maya city in the lowland rainforest. You'll make your "jadeite" out of green Sculpey clay. Sculpey clay is safe to handle, but you should not use your cooking or eating utensils for making and baking the clay. *The clay requires baking, so have an adult supervise.*

1 Notice that the Maya necklace pictured here is made of a mixture of round and long beads. It also contains a large rectangular-shaped decorative centerpiece. You will make all these pieces from clay before you assemble your necklace.

2 Prepare your workspace by covering a table in newspaper. Lie down enough wax paper to give you room to roll out your beads. Or roll out your clay on a glazed tile.

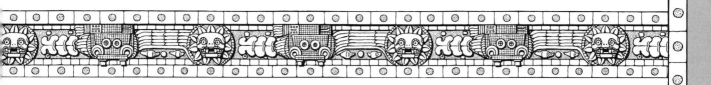

3 Measure out a piece of elastic thread that is long enough for the centerpiece to sit below your collarbone. Remember to add a couple of inches of extra elastic thread on each end to tie the knot (about 5 centimeters). Use the masking tape to tape both ends of the thread piece to your workspace. It will show you how many beads to make. You'll need a few extra beads to hang from the bottom of your centerpiece.

4 Decide which color of clay you want to use. Mix them, if you like. Green with half as much black makes dark green. Equal amounts of green and white makes light green. Or you can use pearl white to make pearl green. After choosing your colors, make your beads. Make round beads by rolling a small piece of clay in the palms of your hands. To make long beads, roll a piece of clay into a smooth ball. Shape the ball into a long log. Roll this log on your wax paper or ceramic tile to make a long coil. Press gently so it remains even. Cut the beads into the desired lengths.

5 Carefully poke holes through the beads with a toothpick. So that you don't crush the bead, poke the toothpick halfway through from one side, then halfway through from the other side, then all the way through. Make sure the hole is large enough for the skewers to fit through easily.

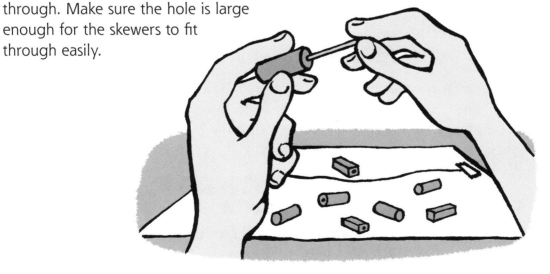

Activity continued on next page . . .

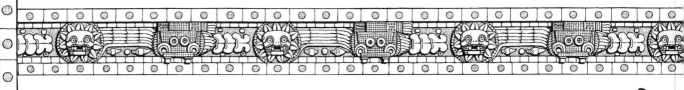

6 To make the rectangular centerpiece bead, draw a T-shaped pattern on an index card and cut it out. Roll out a ¼-inch-thick piece of clay big enough for this piece (½ centimeter thick). Place the pattern on the clay and cut away any extra clay. Cut a "T" shape into the center of the piece, making it as large as you like. Use a toothpick to make holes in the top and bottom corners.

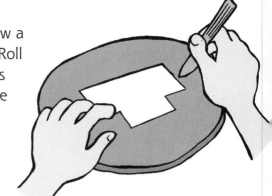

7 Cut slots on both sides of the long sides of the foil pan. Thread the beads onto the wooden skewers and lay the skewers in the slots. Put your bead centerpiece on an index card and place it in the foil pan. The card keeps it from sticking.

8 Bake according to the directions on the clay's packaging. Most polymer clays are baked at 275 degrees Fahrenheit (130 degrees Celsius). Remember that Sculpey clay does NOT harden until it is completely cool.

9 When your pieces are cool, thread the elastic through the top holes in your centerpiece so the elastic runs across the back. With the centerpiece in the middle, add an equal number of beads to each side. When you get to the end of the thread, tie the ends together.

10 Cut two more pieces of elastic thread to hang from the bottom of the necklace. Thread each through one of the bottom holes. When it is even on both sides, add more beads and tie a knot to secure the beads.

DID YOU KNOW?

Many artists were members of Maya royal families, and they often signed their names on their work. In fact, the Maya represent the only Mesoamerican culture in which artists took credit for their individual pieces.

GLOSSARY

agave: a type of cactus plant that grows in Mexico and Central America. The Maya used it for its sisal fibers.

ancestor: a person from your family who lived before you.

aqueduct: a pipe or channel designed to transport water by force of gravity from one place to another.

archaeologist: someone who studies ancient people and their cultures.

astrological: relating to movement of the planets, moon, and stars.

bedrock: the solid rock earth, well beneath the softer surface of soil, sand, clay, gravel, or water.

behead: to cut off a head.

cacao: beans containing seeds that are used to make cocoa, cocoa butter, and chocolate.

capstone: the final, topmost stone in a corbel arch, which joins the sides and completes the structure.

city-state: a city and its surrounding area that rules itself.

civilization: a community of people with a highly developed culture and social organization.

codice: an ancient writing in book form.

colonist: a new settler in an area who is originally from somewhere else.

commoner: an ordinary person without rank or title.

conch shell: a large spiral shell that can be used as a horn.

conquistador: a sixteenth-century Spanish soldier.

copal: a kind of sap that comes from tropical trees that is used in candles.

corbel arch: an arch shaped like an upside-down V that is formed by a series of overlapping stones with each stone jutting out farther toward the center than the one below it. The space left at the end is bridged by a capstone.

crop: plants grown for food and other uses.

curassow: a long-tailed, crested bird that is found in Central and South America.

currency: money or other valuable item used for exchange.

debt: a service or money owed.

demon: an evil spirit.

distinctive: special or unique.

drought: a long period of little or no rain.

dung: solid waste.

epigrapher: someone who studies ancient writings.

fasting: to eat very little or nothing at all. The Maya usually did this for religious purposes.

fetish: a small figurine believed to have magical or spiritual powers.

flint: a very hard, grayish-black form of quartz.

forgery: a copy, not the original.

GLOSSARY

fresco: a work of art painted with pigment on wet plaster on a wall or ceiling.

gnarled: twisted and deformed.

gourd: the dried and hollowed-out shell of plants related to the pumpkin, squash, and cucumber.

haab or Vague Year: the 365-day year of the Maya calendar.

headdress: an elaborate covering for the head worn during ceremonial occasions.

hearth: the floor of a fire or oven.

hieroglyphics: a type of writing system that uses pictures and symbols called hieroglyphs (or just glyphs) to represent words and ideas.

horoscope: a prediction of a person's future based on the position of the planets and stars.

indigo: a blue dye made from the indigo plant.

jadeite: a rare and prized mineral, usually emerald to light green.

laborer: someone who works with his or her hands.

latex: a milky fluid found in many plants.

limestone: a kind of rock the Maya used to build roads, temples, and other important buildings.

logogram: a written character that represents a meaning or word.

loincloth: a strip of cloth worn around the midsection of the body.

Long Count: a complex calendar only used by Maya priests and scribes.

luxury: something that is nice to have but is not necessary.

maize: corn.

majestic: of impressive beauty.

malaria: a painful tropical disease caused by mosquito bites.

mortar: a building material that hardens when it dries. It is used to hold bricks and stones together like glue.

multiple: a number that can be divided evenly by another number.

nomads: a group of people who move in search of food and water.

obsidian: a black glass produced by erupting volcanoes.

pagan: someone who worships many gods, or who has little or no religion.

pelt: an animal skin.

plentiful: available in large amounts.

plumb bob: a weight on the end of a line, used especially by builders to establish exact vertical and horizontal lines.

Pok-A-Tok: a ball game in which teams acted out the ongoing battle between good and evil.

polytheist: a person who believes in more than one god.

GLOSSARY

portable: able to be carried around easily.

procession: a group of people moving along in the same direction, to the same place, or for the same reason.

prominent: important.

prophecy: a prediction of the future.

puberty: when a child's body transitions into an adult body.

purity: innocence or freedom from guilt or evil.

quarry: to dig or cut rock from the earth.

quetzal bird: a bird prized by Maya kings for its brilliant blue-green feathers. Today this bird faces extinction.

raid: attack.

reservoir: a natural or artificial pond or lake used to store and regulate the supply of water.

rival: a competitor.

sacrifice: an offering to a god.

scribe: a member of Maya society who wrote with hieroglyphs on many types of surfaces, as well as in codices, to keep records of all kinds.

shaman-priest: a priest-doctor in Maya society who tended to the physical needs of the people.

sisal: stiff fibers from the agave leaves used by the Maya to make rope and for weaving.

spindle whorl: a rod or pin, narrow at one end and weighted at the other, on which fibers are spun into thread and then wound.

stela: a vertical slab of stone that the Maya used to record dates and important information about their rulers. Most are between 3 and 23 feet tall (1 to 7 meters). Maya artists carved symbols into the stone (plural is stelae).

stucco: a durable finish for exterior walls, usually made of a mixture of cement, sand, limestone, and water, that is applied while wet.

terrace: a level area cut into a steep slope to provide a flat section to plant crops.

trance: a sleeplike state.

tropics: near the equator.

tumpline: a sling for carrying a load on the back, with a strap that passes around the forehead.

tzolk'in or Sacred Round: a period of 260 days constituting a complete cycle of all the combinations of 20 day names with the numbers 1 to 13 that constitutes the Maya sacred year.

underworld: the home of the dead, as well as some of the evil gods.

RESESOURCES

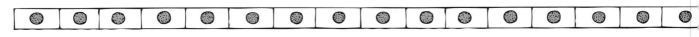

Books

Ancona, George. *Mayeros: A Yucatec Maya Family*. New York: Lothrop, Lee & Shepard Books, 1997.

Coulter, Laurie. *Secrets in Stone: All About Maya Hieroglyphs*. Ontario: Little, Brown and Company, 2001.

Day, Nancy. *Your Travel Guide to Ancient Mayan Civilization*. Minneapolis, MN: Runestone Press, 2001.

Gerson, Mary-Joan. *People of Corn: A Mayan Story*. Ontario: Little, Brown and Company, 1995.

Kallen, Stuart. *The Mayans*. San Diego: Lucent Books, Inc., 2001.

Laughton, Timothy. *The Maya: Life, Myth and Art*. London: Duncan Baird Publishers, 1998.

Lourie, Peter. *The Mystery of the Maya: Uncovering the Lost City of Palenque*. Honesdale, PA: Boyds Mill Press, Inc., 2001.

Macdonald, Fiona. *Step into the Aztec and Mayan Worlds*. London: Lorenze Books, 1998.

Morton, Lyman. *Yucatán Cook Book: Recipes and Tales*. Santa Fe, NM: Red Crane Books, Inc., 1996.

Netzley, Patricia. *Maya Civilization*. San Diego: Lucent Books, Inc., 2002.

Orr, Tamra. *The Maya*. Danbury, CT: Watts Library, 2005.

Polin, C. J. *The Story of Chocolate*. New York: DK Publishing, Inc., 2005.

Sharer, Robert J. *Daily Life in Maya Civilization*. Westport, CT: Greenwood Press, 1996.

Schuman, Michael A. *Mayan and Aztec Mythology*. Berkeley Heights, NJ: Enslow Publishers, Inc., 2001.

Whitlock, Ralph. *Everyday Life of the Maya*. New York: Dorsett Press, 1976.

Web Sites

Jaguar Sun: By Jeeni Criscenzo, author of a novel about the Maya called Place of Mirrors. **www.jaguar-sun.com**

Mayan Kids: Extensive glossary of Maya words. **mayankids.com/mmkglossary/!glossary_h.htm**

Native American Indian Resources: Traditional Maya tales. **www.kstrom.net/isk/maya/mayastor.html**

PBS: **www.pbs.org/wgbh/nova/maya**

Science Museum of Minnesota's Maya Adventure: Chiapas Maya currently living in Mexico. **www.smm.org/sln/ma/chiapas.html**

INDEX

INDEX